CERCA

BY DEBORAH WALL

cerca 1. *adv.* near(by), close; near; etc. at close range
CERCA *prop. n.* a magazine devoted to celebrating places near Las Vegas, particularly those of natural beauty

---

GREAT HIKES

The woman who wrote it

Author Deborah Wall's parents loved the outdoors and shared that love with their children. "My mother used to show us a sample of some specific kind of rock, and the sibling who found one like it, first, was the big winner," Wall said. "By the end of the day we would have climbed a mountain looking for it, which was her intention." Wall has been hiking mountains ever since, first in her native New England, and now in the Southwest.

Wall started writing a book with motives much like her parents had: To show her three daughters the joy of hiking. Because her geographic area of interest had become the region surrounding Las Vegas and extending into three other states — the same country celebrated in *Cerca* publications — Stephens Press agreed to publish that book as the third in its series of *Cerca Country Guides.*

Wall and the editors chose the most interesting and photogenic hikes the region affords, some from each of its four states. This book will conduct you through Utah's Fairyland Loop, up little-known trails in Nevada's Spring Mountains and Sheep Mountains, to Lava Falls on the Colorado River in Arizona, and to California's Hole-in-the-Wall and Joshua Tree National Monument.

Formerly a TV writer and producer, Wall has published articles in *Cerca, Nevada Magazine,* and the *Las Vegas Review-Journal.* She also was a ski racer and has taught skiing as well as sailing. Wall lives in Southern Nevada.

This guide also introduces a new style of maps. The new maps will employ symbols consistently so that a single key, printed on this page, will apply to every map. Mileage scales also have been added to most maps.

A.D. HOPKINS
EDITOR, CERCA

Author Deborah Wall in the mountains.

MAP KEY:

Interstates, U.S. highways	
	Year-round stream/river
State highways	
	National park, state park, wilderness area
Paved secondary roads, streets	
	Government or military installation
Unpaved, gravel or drivable roads	
Four-wheel drive roads	Trailhead
Foot/horse trails	

CERCA
COUNTRY GUIDES

PRESIDENT
Sherman R. Frederick

VICE PRESIDENT/CHIEF OPERATING OFFICER
Michael Ferguson

PUBLISHER
Carolyn Hayes Uber
► cuber@stephenspress.com, (702) 387-5260

EDITOR
A.D. Hopkins
► adhopkins@stephenspress.com, (702) 383-0270

DIRECTOR OF PHOTOGRAPHY
Jim Laurie
► jlaurie@stephenspress.com, (702) 383-0253

ART DIRECTOR
Ched Whitney
► ched@reviewjournal.com

CERCA GREAT HIKES AUTHOR: Deborah Wall
COPY EDITOR: Monica Miceli
PAGE DESIGNER: Paul Doyle
MAP DESIGNER: Mike Johnson

CONTRIBUTORS: Lin Alder, Mark Andrews, Michael Clark, Jim K. Decker, Bruce Griffin, Kerrick James, James Kay, Gary Ladd, Alan Roberts, Frank Serafini, Larry Ulrich.

SUBSCRIPTIONS: Subscriptions to *Cerca Country Guides* are sold by and are the sole responsibility of Mountain Distributors, Inc., Reno, Nevada. All subscriptions inquiries should be sent to:
Mountain Distributors
316 California Avenue, #712
Reno NV 89509
(Toll Free) (877) 686-3478
www.mountaindistributors.com

Copyright 2004 © Stephens Press, LLC.
Cerca County Guides are published by Stephens Press, LLC, Post Office Box 1600, Las Vegas, NV 89125-1600. The opinions and observations expressed in *Cerca* and *Cerca Country Guides* are those of the authors and do not necessarily reflect the opinions of the *Las Vegas Review-Journal,* Stephens Press, LLC or Stephens Media Group.

Wall, Deborah.

Great hikes : a Cerca country guide / by Deborah Wall.
-- Las Vegas, NV : Stephens Press, 2004.

p. ; cm.
(Cerca country guides)

ISBN: 1-932173-28-5

1. Trails--Southwest, New. 2. Southwest, New--Guidebooks.
3. Southwest, New--Description and travel. 4. West (U.S.)--Guidebooks.
5. West (U.S.)--Description and travel. I. Title.

Stephens Press LLC

PO BOX 1600
LAS VEGAS NV 89125
www.stephenspress.com

Printed in Hong Kong

GREAT HIKES

A CERCA COUNTRY GUIDE

BY DEBORAH WALL

The trail leads through five tunnels originally needed to access Boulder Dam — now called Hoover Dam — with construction materials.

RAILROAD
TUNNEL TRAIL

A relic of dam-building days becomes a picturesque and easy excursion

PHOTOGRAPHY BY JIM LAURIE

Lake Mead's man-made beauty contrasts with a brutal natural landscape.

Not surprisingly, the Historic Railroad Tunnel Trail is one of the most popular winter destinations in the Lake Mead National Recreational area, an area of almost one-and-a-half million acres. Laid out along the only remaining intact segment of the once-active Boulder Dam Construction Railroad system, the journey includes five historic tunnels, sweeping views of Lake Mead and surrounding country, as well as easy, gradually-rising terrain and mild winter weather.

My companion on this hike was my daughter Charlotte, only seven years old but already a veteran of a dozen trips along this trail. As an infant she had made the trip kangaroo-style in a Snugli front pack, then graduated to a child-carrier backpack. When she became too heavy for me to haul, I pushed her along in a jogging stroller. Yet today would be a milestone for her, as she planned to do the trail on a mountain bike. I would be on foot and hopefully this would keep us about even with one another on an outing of more than five miles.

From the trailhead parking area, we headed out on an old auto road until we reached a large metal gate, standing open, about five minutes later. Beyond the gate the trail widened, and we were now on a fifteen-foot-wide gravel path that once served as the railroad bed.

Because steam trains worked best on the level or very gradual grades, railroad surveyors picked routes accordingly, so trails built on abandoned railbeds are very pleasant and easy to hike. The entire trail would afford us outstanding views of Lake Mead as we traveled along the base of volcanic cliffs. Although I have seen many different moods of this lake, today it appeared as a sheet of glass only broken by a few small pleasure boats enjoying the cool fall weather

As I walked along behind Charlotte, I thought about the powerful history of this area. It was a desolate place until 1931, when the U.S. Government embarked on the biggest construction project in the world, the building of the Boulder Dam (now called the Hoover Dam). In 1931 the U.S. Government and a group of six western firms, called Six Companies Inc., joined forces to build three rail segments, altogether some 30 miles of standard-gauge 90-pound rail, connecting cement mixing plants, quarry pits, and other facilities needed for dam construction. When in full operation, it required nine steam locomotives and four more that ran on gasoline, and 71 workers.

Desert Princess, a commercial day cruiser, paddles past the Boulder Islands. Though islands are always visible, the waterline is much lower than normal because of an extended drought.

After the dam was completed in 1935, most of the railroad tracks were either flooded over or dismantled, except for the U.S. Government Railroad, the section that we were on. This segment originally ran from Boulder City down Hemenway Wash to Himix, the concrete mixing plant located on the rim of Black Canyon. In 1961 there was one final delivery of a generator to be used at the dam's power plant. Then the tracks were dismantled, removed and sold as scrap in 1962.

After about a half-mile we found a steep spur trail on our right that leads up the left side of a large wash below the Hacienda Hotel and Casino. This is the east parking area where scenic helicopter rides, over Lake Mead and Hoover Dam, are now offered. This section of the old railroad is where a portion of the movie "The Gauntlet" was filmed. Coincidentally, in that part of the movie, an assassin in a helicopter

As on other trails built on former railroad grades, elevation gains and losses are very gradual.

was pursuing Clint Eastwood and Sondra Locke, who were on a motorcycle.

About a quarter-mile before reaching the first tunnel, and down a steep ravine to the right of the railroad bed, we saw the massive concrete plugs removed from the dam to install turbines. They've been lying here abandoned for almost 70 years, I told Charlotte, who seemed little interested in the history lesson. She only had eyes for the tunnel entrance. All the tunnels are about 25 feet in diameter, 300 feet in length — built oversized to accommodate the wide loads such as the penstock sections and large equipment needed to build the dam

When we reached the first tunnel, Charlotte was a little apprehensive about going into the darkness alone, and stopped before the entrance to wait for me. I headed in, and she soon ventured in behind me walking her bike. After making it through with no problems she didn't even stop for me on the next four, which came in rapid succession. We ventured in one, out the next, and so on until the fifth and final tunnel. About 40 feet after the last tunnel, a barbed wire fence, bearing a sign reading "RESTRICTED AREA NO TRESPASSING," blocks further progress.

This tunnel happens to be directly beneath the Lakeview Scenic Overlook, a drive-in viewpoint located about 1.5 miles from the dam. However, do not try to access the tunnel or trail from the overlook. The climb is too steep and dangerous.

This tunnel was sealed after arsonists burned its timbers in 1978, but was restored and reopened in July 2001.

Although plans had been in the works to have the trail continue past this tunnel and go all the way to the dam, that plan is on hold indefinitely in the high-security climate that now prevails around important structures.

After leaving the last tunnel for our return to the trailhead, Charlotte asked if we could come back tomorrow. I said yes, but by the time we were back at the car she was tired, had changed her mind, and wanted to know a little more about the helicopter rides.◆

Jim Laurie is the director of photography for Stephens Press and Cerca. *He is himself a dedicated hiker.*

Getting there

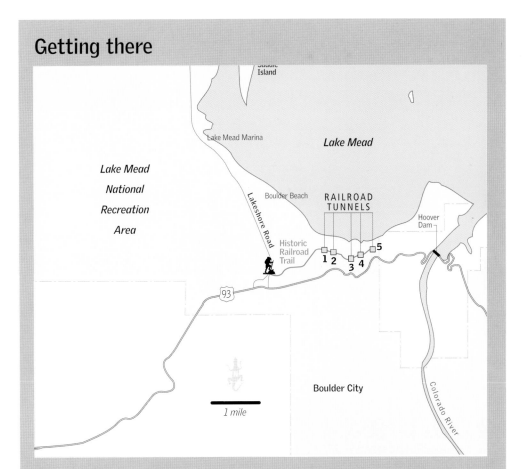

Location: Railroad Tunnel Trail in the Lake Mead National Recreation Area, about 30 miles from Las Vegas.

Directions: Take U.S. Highway 93 south past Boulder City to the Lake Mead National Recreation Area. Go left on Lakeshore Road and drive .4 mile, parking in the signed trailhead parking area, on the right .1 mile past the Alan Bible Visitor Center.

Difficulty: Easy.

Length: 5.2 miles round trip from the trailhead to the fifth tunnel.

Elevation at trailhead: 1,600 feet.

Elevation gain: Minimal.

Water: Bring your own.

Hazards: Although this is a wide trail, there are dangerous cliffs and drop-offs along a few sections. Open mines near trail. Severe heat in summer.

Season: November through April. Mornings or late evenings during the warmer months. If you must do it in summer, head out at dawn. Temperatures are commonly 10 degrees higher than in Las Vegas, and at midday can exceed 120 in the shade.

Topographic maps: Trails Illustrated — Lake Mead National Recreation Area. For more detail, use U.S.G.S. Boulder Beach (1:24,000). Available at the Alan Bible Visitor Center.

Lake Mead National Recreation Area: Open year-round. Vehicle entrance fee is $5, good for 5 days. However, the Railroad Tunnel Trailhead is located before the entrance, so there is no need to pay the fee. Visitor Center is open daily 8:30 a.m.-4:30 p.m. daily, except Thanksgiving, Christmas, and New Year's Day. (702) 293-8990, **www.nps.gov/lame/.**

A silhouetted hiker with a walking stick treks along the Virgin River's edge.
(JAMES KAY)

Narrow Escape

The best Zion has to offer provides the perfect getaway

PHOTOGRAPHY BY JAMES KAY AND ALAN ROBERTS

Canyoneering adventures, even simple ones, are always filled with surprises, humbling challenges, and geologic wonders. And if you hike sixteen miles in one day, through the Zion Narrows, you start to understand why this trip has been called the best hike in the American West.

Our journey was physically demanding; we made hundreds of river crossings, struggled with algae-covered rocks, took many falls, and at times got extremely cold and weary. Yet we got to float in dark pools below cascading springs, stood under flowing waterfalls, and explored hidden side chasms, all surrounded by pink sandstone alcoves, arches, and overhangs within one of the most famous canyons in the world.

This adventure would start outside the eastern boundary of Zion National Park and take us down the North Fork of the Virgin River. It is one of the most difficult ways to do the trip; most people start from the park's Riverside Walk, hike upstream to the Narrows, and turn around. Others use the through route we did, but camp in the canyon to rest a night.

My hiking partner and I set out from Chamberlain's Ranch just before an extremely cool and overcast dawn. We were prepared, but far from overconfident. Could we make our trip safely? Would we get stranded? Did we forget anything? And as we closed the gate and watched our shuttle and its driver disappear into darkness, it occurred to me that the only person who could help us was speeding away on a forty-mile-long road.

Between the two of us, we have made dozens of canyoneering trips around the Southwest, exploring slot canyons, rappelling waterfalls, swimming, and discovering places unknown to all but a few. Canyoneering has surged in popu-

There are some paths along the riverbanks but they are short, often lead nowhere, and back into the water you go.

larity the last few years, not only as part of a trend toward adventure sports, but also because new and better gear makes canyoneering feasible year round, while better means of forecasting weather, especially flash floods, reduces the risk.

Although our route required no technical climbing, its length required plenty of preparation: Obtaining a complete dry suit apiece, getting a back country permit from the National Park Service, arranging for a shuttle to meet us at five a.m., even packing a reliable alarm clock to wake us at four a.m. in time to eat a quick breakfast. We also needed luck: A clear twenty-four-hour weather report with no flash flood potential, a water flow under 120 cubic feet per second, and dry conditions on the access road. If fortune or foresight failed us on even one count, the trip would be off.

But all fell into place. After a ninety-minute drive from the Zion Canyon Visitor Center we were on our way. The first stretch gave no hint of the effort to come. We walked a jeep trail through a sage-covered valley next to the meandering North Fork. In this setting of open meadows, wildflowers, and pine trees, we came to Bulloch's Cabin, a two-story abode of hand-hewn logs, now abandoned with its roof on the verge of collapse.

Soon after Bulloch's Cabin, the jeep trail became a well-worn cattle path along the river. Maple trees, aspens, and conifers grow here, and the area's signature Navajo sandstone appeared when the route became more canyonlike. As the canyon walls became higher and closer, we eventually had to make our first of hundreds of river crossings. The ankle-deep water was almost unbearably cold. Throughout this section, we had to climb over or under many fallen trees. Soon we came to a thirty-foot-long logjam. Commonly found in tight canyons, these can easily become ankle-breakers, but we got over it safely.

The canyon's walls were closer and closer together as we moved down-

THIS PAGE:
With water waist deep in many areas, Zion Narrows requires proper equipment and thorough planning before hikers attempt this sixteen-mile trek.
(JAMES KAY)

PREVIOUS PAGE:
Spectacular scenery and majestic cliffs await hikers on the Virgin River through the Zion Narrows on what many have deemed the best hike in the American West.
(ALAN ROBERTS)

Narrow Escape

stream and the light played tricks; many times we couldn't tell which way the canyon really headed, and we made false starts in the wrong direction. Three hours into the trip we found a small yellow sign that marked the national park boundary. Soon after we came upon a twelve-foot waterfall. This could have been a major obstacle, but a four-foot-wide cleft, on the left, brought us down and past the fall. We found it worth the effort to walk back up and see it close, pouring into a deep, dark pool.

There is nothing like it in the world. Walls only twenty feet apart tower as high as 1,500 feet.

We traveled downriver through many other intense, narrow areas, before the canyon opened up again at its confluence with Deep Creek. This creek adds sixty percent more water to North Fork. After Deep Creek the river turns south, and we stopped for lunch and a rest.

When we resumed our journey, we noticed the rocks in the river had slippery algae that slowed our progress. We needed to rely on our walking sticks for every step. Later, Ron Terry, public information officer at Zion National Park, explained why. "Higher up the river there is less sediment carried in the water and here there is a greater volume of water. It's more conducive to buildup on rocks."

Not many years ago, this area was seldom seen. For most of the year the frigid water, with its threat of hypothermia, kept hikers out of the narrowest and most dramatic parts of the canyon. It was more popular in hot summer months, but then hikers sometimes headed blindly up the canyon into flash floods. Every year there are twenty to thirty such surges from thunderstorms, Terry said. "We post a flash flood potential and work with people based on that information." He added, "Permits are not issued if the CFS is 120 or stronger and we try to discourage people if it is close to that."

THIS PAGE: Waterfalls, algae-covered rocks, and slippery river crossings challenge hikers along the trek through the Narrows.
(JAMES KAY)

NEXT PAGE: Hiking permits are regulated by the National Park Service and depend on the water level of the river.
(ALAN ROBERTS)

Narrow Escape

Because the water was so cold, and the slippery rocks increased our chances of falling in, we donned dry suits. These were a mixed blessing. They do prevent hypothermia, but the rubber gasket that seals the neck of my suit is so tight that pulling it over the head usually involves hair loss. My suit has a back zipper that I cannot zip or unzip by myself. And since I drank nearly three gallons of water in ten hours on this strenuous trip, all my rest stops involved the lengthy process of getting out of the suit, then suiting up once more.

We hadn't expected to see another soul until farther downstream, but we soon came upon two young men, one of them stark naked. We had appeared unexpectedly as they changed into dry clothes. Red-faced, this man grabbed some cover, and we talked for a few minutes. They had just finished the

With the right gear, proper orientation from professionals, and modern technology in forecasting storms, it is possible to see this place in relative safety.

highly technical Kolob Creek canyoneering route, which includes over ten rappels, some more than one hundred feet.

As we headed downstream from Kolob Creek, the deeper water slowed our progress, and we were getting tired. Soon, though, we recognized the side canyon of Goose Creek. Years ago, we had come down this canyon from Zion's Kolob Terrace, so it was familiar

territory, and seeing it boosted our morale. (It's worth the short walk up the bottom of the Narrows just to see this slot. You won't be able to venture far without climbing equipment, though.)

Just after Goose we rounded the corner and came upon the luxuriant ferns, moss-covered rocks, and twin waterfalls from Big Springs. Cascading whitewater flowed into deep pools, and we took pleasure in standing under the springs that pour their waters directly into the river.

That was the best part of the trip for me; the next few miles were the hardest. Deep mud, bouldering, and slippery rocks made for very slow going, and stream crossings became a wearying and

A hiker fills water bottles near the lush Big Springs. Filtering the water before drinking is mandatory.
(JAMES KAY)

dangerous process of trial and error. Now the water was often chest deep. There are some paths along the riverbanks but they are short, often lead nowhere, and back into the water you go. We had water-proofed our packs, and in some deep areas were floating down-river, using our hiking staffs for paddles, as the easiest route and the most fun. That felt pretty close to heaven.

We were amazed to see small slate-colored birds, perfectly at home in a canyon so narrow that the sun seems never to shine there. About seven to eight inches long, they scurried from rock to rock, never more than four or five inches from the water surface. They feed on insects, aquatic invertebrates, and small fish, Terry told me. Their feeding behavior, bobbing up and down, has earned them their name: dippers.

Soon we entered the narrow-est section. This is what most people come to experience and there is nothing like it in the world. Walls only twenty feet apart tower as high as 1,500 feet. Jonathan Zampella tried to explain its attraction: "It offers a sense of humility to be surrounded by such geological history and water older than me. It's a far greater place then I am."

When Zampella first visited the region, he vainly sought high and low for a place to rent protective clothing so he could venture farther into the canyon. Purchasing his own gear else-where, he returned to hike the Narrows in comfort. He found it so moving, in 1997 he founded Zion Adventure Company to outfit others for the same experience.

From here on we started seeing day hikers bound upstream in the signature red dry suits from ZAC. We talked briefly with everyone, mostly to answer questions about the distance to Big Springs, and the depth of the water upstream. All said it was their first trip here. Zampella said about twenty-five percent of his customers are from

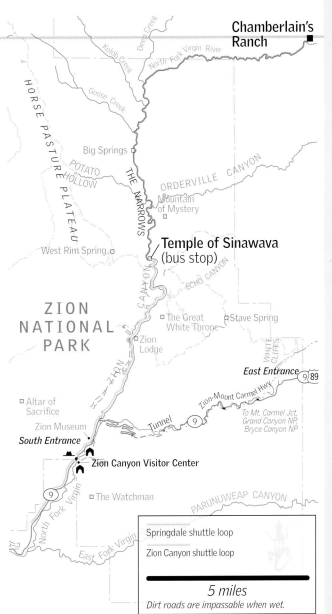

Europe and Asia, and most others from the United States. "With our orientation program people can go in there now and enjoy it. They'll know where they are going and what to look for. We edu-cate people on risks and how to man-age them."

With the right gear, proper orienta-tion from professionals, and modern technology in forecasting storms, it is possible to see this place in relative safe-ty. Everyone I've met who has visited Zion Narrows agrees that it lived up to its reputation: the best hike in the American West.◆

James Kay has traveled the world on photo assignments, but makes his headquarters in Utah's Wasatch Range, and says his favorite photography locations are the canyons of Southern Utah, such as the Narrows.

Alan Roberts has contributed photographs to nearly all Cerca publications since they were launched in 2001. He lives in Las Vegas and the outdoors surrounding it.

Getting there

Location: Zion Narrows, about 145 miles northeast of Las Vegas in Zion National Park, near Springdale, Utah.

Directions: From Las Vegas, take Interstate 15 north 125 miles to Utah Route 9 (Exit 16, or the Hurricane/Zion National Park exit). Drive east 19 miles to Springdale and Zion National Park.

Three ways to hike Zion Narrows
1. Day hike: From the Riverside Walk in Zion's main canyon, walk up river and back. This 4-mile round trip is the easiest way to see the Narrows, no permit required. Some hikers go farther. Because it's mostly wading against the current, time required varies greatly according to that day's water volume.
2. Day hike: From top to bottom (Chamberlain's Ranch Route), 16 miles, permit needed, 10 to 12 hours for well-conditioned hikers.
3. Overnight hike: From top to bottom (Chamberlain's Ranch Route), 16 miles, 12 campsites available, permit and campsite reservation needed.

Directions to Chamberlain's Ranch trailhead: From Zion's east entrance on Utah Route 9 (Mount Carmel Highway), drive 2.4 miles and go left on North Fork Road for 18 miles. Turn left after small bridge and drive a quarter-mile to the Chamberlain's Ranch gate. Snow closes North Fork Road for much of the winter. The Zion Backcountry Desk can give you local road conditions.

Hikers shuttle to Chamberlain's Ranch trailhead: Zion Canyon Transportation, (435) 635-5993, and Springdale Cycles, (435) 772-0575, offer shuttle services to Chamberlain's Ranch, for $25 per hiker. It takes more than an hour one-way, and you must make reservations.

Riverside Walk/Temple of Sinawava: An easy paved mile, it's also the finish line for the downriver hike from Chamberlain's Ranch and starts the day hike upstream to the Narrows.

Best time to go: May through October for through hike. Year-round (with dry suit) for day travel up the Zion Narrows and back from the Riverside Walk. Midsummer and early fall are more prone to flash floods.

Permits: Required for all through hikes and overnight trips from Chamberlain's Ranch into the North Fork, $5 per group. There is a limit of 80 people per day on day hikes and 12 groups overnight.

Outfitters: Zion Adventure Company, 36 Lion Blvd. Springdale, Utah, (435) 772-1001, **www.zionadventures.com.**

Equipment: Dry suit, river shoes, wading staff, and a headlamp. Underneath your dry suit you'll need fleece or other synthetic fabric; do not wear cotton, which has no insulating value if wet. Waterproof pack by lining it with a plastic bag. For overnight or longer day hikes, take a water filter.

Topographic maps: National Geographic Trails Illustrated, Zion National Park 1:37,700, Clear Creek Mountain and Temple of Sinawava 1:24,000. All maps are available at the Zion Visitor Center.

Zion National Park: Entrance fee for auto is $20 and is good for seven days. Shuttle bus is the only access to Riverside Walk/Temple Of Sinawava from April to end of October. For information, contact (435) 772-3256 or **www.nps.gov/zion.** Visitor center at south entrance, in Springdale, Utah, is open 8 a.m. to 7 p.m. daily in summer, shorter hours fall to spring; call the Zion Canyon Backcountry Desk (435) 772-0170.

JIM LAURIE

Don't miss the turnoff, or you'll head for Alamo the hard way

DEBORAH WALL

The cabin at Hidden Forest is voluntarily stocked with emergency supplies by hikers.

JIM LAURIE

A winter evening in the Sheep Mountains, looking southeast.

this cabin door is never locked

Make yourself at home on the Hidden Forest trail; just make sure you leave something behind

Standing at the Hidden Forest Trailhead, surrounded by an open desert landscape with a plant community of small Joshua trees and yucca, it was hard to envision that in a few hours we would be inside a century-old rustic cabin in a snowy ponderosa-and-white-fir forest high in the Sheep Mountains. In just a little more than five miles our route would climb more than 2,000 feet, through three plant communities — blackbrush, pinyon/juniper, and pine/fir forest.

JIM LAURIE

A couple of poles help photographer Jim Decker hike into Hidden Forest. Snowshoes or skis would come in handy.

A friend and I were taking a mid-winter hike in the 1.6-million-acre Desert National Wildlife Range. The refuge was established in 1936 for the preservation and management of the desert bighorn sheep, and is the largest wildlife refuge in the continental United States. Yet, when we arrived at the refuge's main entrance, Corn Creek Field Station, we signed the log book and noticed we were the only ones signed up, that day or in the past few, to hike anywhere outside the Corn Creek area. In an area more than twice the size of Rhode Island, that's a privacy level of which most hikers only dream.

From here we drove eighteen miles on a gravel road, all within the wildlife range, to reach the trailhead. There, a sign reads that Wiregrass Spring is four miles away, but don't believe it. The cabin is five miles up the trail, and the spring, which everybody wants to reach, is several hundred yards past that.

We headed down a rocky slope into a wide wash, went right and found another gate that marked the beginning of Deadman's Canyon. A steady elevation gain over the next mile brought us into a more canyon-like setting and then into a pinyon-juniper woodland.

About two miles into the hike, we reached the first snowy patches on the trail. We had presumed we would see a bit of snow in the higher elevations, but as we continued up the canyon we were surprised to find up to a foot on the ground. Unwisely, we had left our snowshoes in the car. Soon we were traveling at a snail's pace, not knowing if we were still on the trail.

Taking a rest on a four-foot-thick fallen ponderosa tree, we caught our first glimpse of the cabin, and after some ten minutes more of trudging through the snow, we were finally there.

The wood building is set on a small rise, and was in great shape compared to other cabins I have seen out in the wilds. Roof, windows, chimney pipe and door were all intact.

This federally-owned cabin was added to the National Register of Historic Places in 1975. Its exact construction date is unknown, but according to the National Register's nomination form, it is probably the work of a miner or cattleman about the end of the nineteeth century, give or take a few years. The nomination reads, "The hand hewn lumber construction and isolated location embodies the self-reliance and endurance of the first Euro-Americans to penetrate Nevada's backcountry." Moonshiners also used the cabin during Prohibition.

These days the cabin is solely a destination for hikers, and so well stocked you could live in it for weeks. When we visited, the inventory included a wood stove, a day's supply of dry wood, an ax, a hammer, various sizes of pots and pans, canned and dried food, matches, a dining table, a broom, a tent, a sleeping bag, photographs and plenty of reading material. It seems that here, visitors have revived the old-fashioned but admirable backcountry tradition of leaving something useful. In the past, the custom sometimes saved lives, and nearly always made the next visitor feel more kindly toward humanity.

Just outside the cabin's front door, there were two wooden picnic tables, a thermometer, a hummingbird feeder, and even a football. We threw the football back and forth a few times until it deflated, and took some photos with it because we happened to know the Las Vegas hiker who left it there.

Around back there were rusty old chimney pipes and a spare wood stove. Nearby there was a small corral, complete with a fancy wrought-iron gate.

Wiregrass Spring is located less than a quarter-mile uphill from the cabin, but because of the heavy snow we didn't venture up. The U.S. Fish and Wildlife Service told me there is water available year-round from the spring, but added that it may contain bacterial contaminants. It must be treated before human consumption, they warned.

On departure we left a fresh pack of AA batteries we didn't need, hoping they might light up the darkness for some future visitor. If you come, think about what you might not need, and if another could possibly use it, leave it.

Anyone have a spare pair of snowshoes? ◆

Getting there

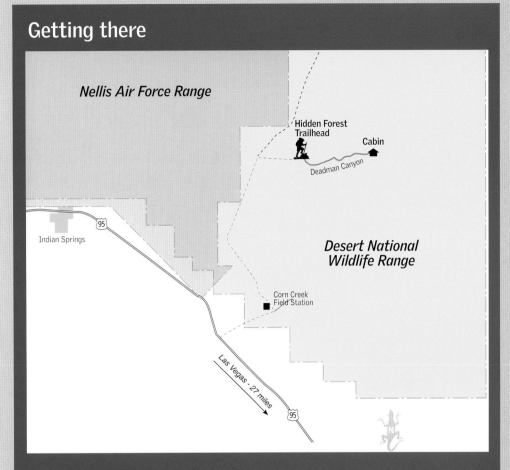

Location: Hidden Forest Trail in Desert National Wildlife Refuge, starts 47 miles from Las Vegas.

Directions: From Las Vegas go north on U.S. 95 for 27 miles. Go right onto Corn Creek Road for 2 miles to Corn Creek Field Station. Go left 14.4 miles on Alamo Road to Hidden Forest Road. Go right 3.6 miles to parking area and trailhead.

Season: October to May, snow in upper reaches in winter.

Length: 10.2 miles round trip.

Elevation at trailhead: 5,860 ft.

Elevation gain: 2,090 ft.

Difficulty: Strenuous.

Water: Bring your own.

Hazards: Flash floods. Heavy snow in winter.

Camping: No fees, but sign in at the Corn Creek Field Station. The cabin is available first come, first served. Camping near the cabin is also allowed, and dispersed camping in other parts of the range, except within one-quarter mile of water sources.

Desert National Wildlife Range: No fee, but sign in at the Corn Creek Field Station. All roads in the DNWR are worn gravel passages and require a high-clearance vehicle. (702) 879-6110, desertcomplex.fws.gov.

Services: No fuel or service is available within the DNWR.

Topographic maps: BLM-Nevada Indian Springs 1:100,000. For more detail use USGS 1:24,000 for Hayford Peak and Sheep Peak. Available at the DNWR Offices, 4701 N. Torrey Pines Drive, Las Vegas, (702) 515-5450.

HIKING

Looking north into Bryce Canyon from near Sunrise Point, a few minutes after sunset.

PHOTOGRAPHY BY ALAN ROBERTS

Bryce Canyon's Fairyland Loop

the HOODOOS

Morning at Tower Bridge; it's usually seen from a trail on the other side.

Standing on the eastern escarpment of the Paunsaugunt Plateau in Bryce Canyon National Park, I looked down into the horseshoe-shaped amphitheater. Before me were hundreds of fragile-looking natural pillars, pinnacles, and spires known as hoodoos. The light pastel colors of this landscape were dreamlike and created a gentle under-pinning for a view to the east — a view reaching more than 100 miles. Bryce is out of this world, and it's completely appropriate that one of its major trails is named Fairyland Loop.

Longer by miles than most day hikes in Bryce, it would be well worth the extra effort to get the outstanding views and the solitude it offered me. Although the trail would take me over eight miles, with an elevation gain and loss of more than 2,000 feet, the topography became so different from anything I had hiked

before, so surreal, that I passed through it as if in a dream, without any sense of effort.

It helped that I was hiking in late April. While other parts of the Southwest were already warm with springtime flowers in bloom, here at an elevation of around 8,000 feet, the nights were still in the twenties and daytime highs in the fifties. There were even snow patches. I consider those ideal hiking conditions – you can hike as fast as you like without getting overheated or having to search for shade, and if you get cold, you can always put on a jacket.

Bryce National Park was established in 1928. Now, more than 1.5 million people visit yearly to hike, sightsee, and photograph this unique place. In the winter months, when snow blankets the canyon, cross-country skiing and

snowshoeing are popular along Bryce's rim trail and the plateau through its ponderosa forests and meadows. In fact, the access road to the trailhead is closed in winter to vehicles and open only to those who make their way to the rim by skis, snowshoes, or perhaps, knee boots.

The hike makes a large loop around Boat Mesa, which divides Fairyland and Campbell Canyons, the main drainages of this hike. The trail is signed and easy to follow. From the trailhead the path made a swift and steep descent into Fairyland Canyon. Looking at the hoodoos from the rim was fascinating, but it was positively intense to stand face to face with them. I say face to face because the imagination tends to run wild here, seeing faces, animals. and cartoon characters carved by erosion in the soft rock.

Photographer Alan Roberts on the trail near Fairyland Canyon.

Most of the shapes seemed pleasing, but some were grotesque and eerie, changing before my eyes as I walked past and viewed them from a different angle and light. Down here in the canyon of mystery, it's easy to see how the geological term for such a fantastically shaped formation, "hoodoo," was adapted from an earlier one meaning "voodoo" or "a person or thing that causes bad luck."

But hoodoos have the fascination of Halloween: a little scary and a lot of fun. In fact, being down in the canyon, among the hoodoos and far from human help, is the joy of the hike.

There are also other natural formations suggesting the works of man, like Boat Mesa, Tower Bridge, and the Chinese Wall. Less than halfway into the hike on my left I could see the delicate formation called Tower Bridge.

Soon after, I found a sign pointing out a 200-foot spur trail that took me to the base of the bridge. It was worth the short trip to see the narrow and horizontal rock that joins two spires.

Back on the main trail it was a steady ascent to the Chinese Wall, one of the grandest formations in the park. Atop a high ridge, this natural cliff looks like a stately fortress, and at its base I found a heavy deposit of snow that the wall guards from the sun. Although this formation looks impenetrable in most parts, in some portions erosion has created holes and windows, and on the outer ends, portions once attached to the wall now stand alone as hoodoos.

After a steep ascent I was back on the Rim Trail, where I headed to my right, or north. The Rim Trail is one of the most popular in the park and travels about 5.5 miles from Fairyland Point to

Bryce Point. I would be on it for just a few miles as I headed back to Fairyland Point to finish my loop. Along the way I passed a few of the sites at North Campground and even found a few people relaxing in camp chairs, soaking up the sun of early spring.

The rim segment provided outstanding views. To the north were Table Cliffs and Aquarius Plateau; to the east, Navajo Mountain, Canaan Peak, and Kaiparowits Plateau. But it didn't give me that doubly alive and surreal feeling I had when walking among the hoodoos. Back in the normal world, I felt a little like Dorothy back in Kansas, at a loss to articulate the wonder that was Oz.◆

Alan Roberts wanders the West with medium-format cameras, capturing photos, which have been published in Plateau Journal, Cerca, *and* calendars.

Getting there

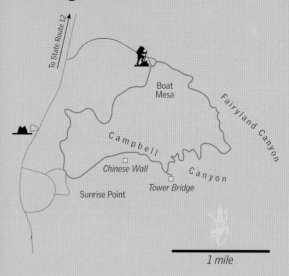

To State Route 12

Boat Mesa

Fairyland Canyon

Campbell

Chinese Wall

Canyon

Tower Bridge

Sunrise Point

1 mile

Location: Bryce Canyon National Park, Utah, about 242 miles northeast of Las Vegas.

Directions: From Las Vegas take Interstate 15 north 125 miles to Utah Route 9 (exit 16-Hurricane/Zion National Park). Follow for 57 miles through Zion and turn left at Mt. Carmel Junction. Take U.S. 89 north for 43 miles to a right onto Utah Route 12. Follow for 14 miles and turn right on Utah Route 63. Travel 3 miles to Bryce Canyon National Park entrance.

Season: April through October.

Length: Loop of 8 miles.

Elevation at trailhead: 8,152 feet.

Difficulty: Moderate.

Elevation gain and loss: 2,309 feet.

Water: Bring your own.

Shuttle services: Free shuttle service with a paid park entrance fee.

Camping: Bryce Canyon National Park has two campgrounds, North and Sunset, with 204 sites available for $10 per night, first-come, first-served. Ruby's Inn Campground has tent sites, tepees, and cabins available from April 1 through November, **www.rubysinn.com.**

Fees: The Fairyland Loop trailhead is located before the park's entrance station. To access the rest of the park it is $20 per vehicle for seven days.

Bryce Canyon National Park: Open all year. **www.nps.gov/brca.** The visitor center is located 1.5 miles inside the entrance station. A short informational video is shown free of charge on the half hour and hour. Open all year except on Thanksgiving, Christmas, and New Year's Day. Ranger staffed information and backcountry desk. (435) 834-5322.

Topographic maps: Trails Illustrated — Bryce Canyon National Park, 1:32,270. For more detail use Bryce Canyon hiking map, 1:10,000. Available at Ruby's Inn and Bryce Canyon National Park Visitor Center.

On this magnificent bluff you can see the narrow parts called "fins" weathering away to become free-standing hoodoos.

close calls at **lava falls**

for a **near-death experience**, try this canyon hike in hot weather

PHOTOGRAPHY BY GARY LADD

Lava cascades pour into the Grand Canyon from the north side of Colorado River, just downstream from Lava Falls.

Bear grass at the edge of the gorge at Toroweap Overlook.

Hiking out of the Grand Canyon on the Lava Falls Route is a challenge under the best circumstances, but hiking it alone on a hot September day, like I did, is just plain dangerous. It wasn't planned to be so, but it became one of the biggest tests of my physical and mental strength I have had while hiking.

My hiking partner, Phil Chrisman, was still down at the river because he was having trouble breathing and couldn't make it back up. He was going to rest and give it another try the next morning with the help of some new friends we had met earlier in the morning. In the meantime, I would hike out and contact the park ranger. If they didn't make it up by noon the next day, I would work on an emergency plan.

The day had started out perfect. Seeing the sun rise over the Grand Canyon that morning was one of the most spectacular sights I had ever encountered, but by the end of the day, seeing it sink out of sight would be my only wish.

We arrived at the trailhead at 6 am. Our plan was to hike down to the river, spend a few hours in the canyon, and with luck see some rafts tackle the infamous Lava Falls. Then we would start the return trip before the heat became too intense.

It was an ambitious undertaking because the terrain was treacherous, and the cool temperatures forecast for the day had not materialized.

We found the trail register different from those encountered at other trailheads in the Southwest. Besides asking your name, where you are from, and the date, it asks if you made it to the river or not. In the last three weeks before our visit, about fifty people had signed the register, but only eight hikers had made it down and back.

The beginning of the route was easy, with an obvious trail. We hiked our way down into a wash, which led into the ominously named Vulture Valley, a bowl-shaped area of red cinders. The wash continued and led us down to the top of a small cliff, a matter of five feet that we carefully climbed down.

From here the terrain changed dramatically. We came upon a barrel cactus standing alone and wondered how it grew here, but just minutes farther along, the lava slope was filled with them. Amid these hundreds of barrel cacti, the route was steep and became hard to find, for the cairns seemed to lead us in many different directions. We picked the most obvious route, and along it we placed frozen liters of Gatorade to drink on the way back, in three different spots, sheltered from the sun behind rocks and cacti.

Arriving at a red cinder formation known as Finger Rock Ridge, we cached another liter of Gatorade, rested, and checked our topographic map.

We skirted around the hill to the left and reached a black lava saddle that rose above our last obstacle. This was a chute, that is, a narrow, steep trough with steep sides that prevent hikers from climbing out onto some alternate route. It gave us a straight shot to the Colorado River about 1,000 feet below, but the way was filled with loose boulders, without a clearly defined trail through them.

It looked bad, but once we started off it was even worse than I thought. Every rock was loose and with each footstep came rockslides. This was a tough and dangerous area and for a time I thought we were not on a route at all, and the cairns were somebody's idea of a cruel joke. We dropped our last Gatorade here and continued down, staying to the right side of the chute, where it was more stable.

Halfway down we had problems. I was about twenty feet below Phil when I heard rocks falling and Phil yelling "Rock!" And

A tangle of basalt columns lies at the base of a cliff a short distance downstream from Lava Falls.

here it came, a two-foot-long boulder rolling and bouncing straight toward me. I jumped out of the way quickly and it went past, missing my leg by inches. I yelled to Phil to stay where he was, until I could find a safe haven from any other rockslides that might start as he continued down.

We were very relieved when we made it safely down to the rivers edge. And our efforts were immediately rewarded with our discovery of two blue rafts tied up, getting ready to try the exciting run through Lava Falls.

Although called "falls," these impressive rapids are really a series of natural, jumbled dams. They were formed by debris washed down from Prospect Canyon, opposite us on the south shore of the river, which is part of the Hualapai Indian Reservation.

We hiked downstream about 300 yards, coming to the rocky bench overlooking the rapids. Two other hikers were here; Utah natives David Bell and Laurie Savage were spending two nights in the canyon. They befriended us immediately.

As we waited for the two rafts to do the falls, David, an ex-river guide, explained the routine rafters follow in approaching the falls. They walk up to the lookout where we were, and from there assess the river and decide how they will handle the rapids. Right on cue, six young men came walking up and did just that. Serious discussion was punctuated by a lot of pointing and nodding before they returned to their rafts.

I watched, spellbound, as the first raft headed downriver toward us, bore to the right, and went into the rapids. It rode the waves easily, and the second raft followed minutes later. I was envious and wished I could have been on board.

Thinking we had seen all the river action that would occur this day, we walked back with David and Laurie to their campsite on the riverbank, where we took a long break in the shade and had our lunch. While we were eating, a dozen kayakers paddled by, a few coming over to the bank and talking with us; they all wondered how we got down to such a remote place. While chatting, we filtered some river water, which was silty and clogged our filter almost immediately. After about thirty minutes of pumping, which put about seventy ounces of water into our drinking bags, we quit. After all, we had established

caches of Gatorade higher up the trail.

It was starting to get warm, and we decided to start back up. I took a swim in the chilly river and felt refreshed and energized. We thanked David and Laurie for sharing their shade and left.

We had only hiked ten minutes, just reaching the base of the chute, when Phil said he couldn't make it back up that day. I took a close look at his face, which had become pale and weary, and knew he was right. Phil was in good physical condition for his sixty years, and a very seasoned hiker to boot. But he had experienced a heart attack several months before, and we both feared, without bespeaking it, that he might be facing another.

This left three choices. He could try to hitch a ride on a raft, which could take days to reach the next take-out spot. We could send word for a helicopter rescue. Or, with a night's rest and some luck, Phil could possibly make it up the next day under his own power. We agreed on a variation of number three: I would go back up alone and alert the rangers that an emergency situation might be developing, while Phil rested a night in camp with David and Laurie. All three would then attempt the climb in the cooler temperatures of morning.

I started up the chute, touching off a few rockslides, and after just ten minutes of climbing I was already searching for shade. There was shade on the right side of the chute, but that was the most dangerous place to be, so I toughed out the heat on the left. Knowing how far I needed to go from here, I started to think I wouldn't make it up either.

With my brains quietly simmering, I couldn't even remember where to find the break in the saddle, which led out of the trap. I hoped the cairns would easily lead me, but discovered these rock piles are not easy to see going up the rocky hill; I needed to look carefully above me every few steps in order to find the next cairn.

I finally made it and was on top of the chute and through the black saddle. I never found the Gatorade we had stashed here, which was all right in the end, because David, Laurie, and Phil would appreciate it tomorrow.

But the next bottle tasted great, ten minutes later at the Finger Rock Ridge.

Yet here, in the only good shade of the hike, my confidence failed. I pon-

Lava Falls drops fourteen feet, not the thirty-seven that many believe, but it's still a treacherous whitewater for river runners.

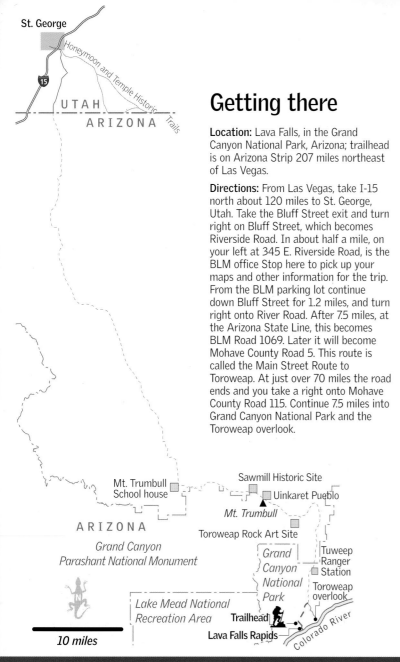

Getting there

Location: Lava Falls, in the Grand Canyon National Park, Arizona; trailhead is on Arizona Strip 207 miles northeast of Las Vegas.

Directions: From Las Vegas, take I-15 north about 120 miles to St. George, Utah. Take the Bluff Street exit and turn right on Bluff Street, which becomes Riverside Road. In about half a mile, on your left at 345 E. Riverside Road, is the BLM office Stop here to pick up your maps and other information for the trip. From the BLM parking lot continue down Bluff Street for 1.2 miles, and turn right onto River Road. After 7.5 miles, at the Arizona State Line, this becomes BLM Road 1069. Later it will become Mohave County Road 5. This route is called the Main Street Route to Toroweap. At just over 70 miles the road ends and you take a right onto Mohave County Road 115. Continue 7.5 miles into Grand Canyon National Park and the Toroweap overlook.

Directions to trailhead: From the Toroweap overlook drive back about 3 miles. Go left on the signed Lava Falls access road. Drive 2.4 miles to the trailhead parking area. Four-wheel drive is necessary the last mile.

Season: October through April, weather permitting.

Length: 1.5 miles

Difficulty: Extremely strenuous on return trip.

Elevation at trailhead: 4,180 feet

Elevation loss: 2,540 feet

Water: Colorado River. Cache water or other liquid on the way down for the return.

Special equipment: Leather gloves and hiking boots with good traction; also water treatment filter or equivalent equipment.

Hazards: Steep scree slopes, rockslides, hard-to-follow route, no shade.

Primitive passages: High-clearance or four-wheel drive vehicles are recommended for the road trip to Toroweap, and they need hard-to-puncture truck or off-road tires. Recreational vehicles, trailers, and low-clearance vehicles of any kind should not attempt this trip. In some weather, snow or mud can make the road impassable. No gas, food, water, lodging, garbage collection, or other services are provided; bring extra gasoline for exploring. Cell phones do not pick up a signal. BLM, which administers most of the Arizona Strip, recommends carrying at least the following emergency equipment: two full-sized spare tires with jack and lug wrench, basic tool kit, plenty of emergency water and food, first aid kit, flashlight, blankets or sleeping bag, and a map.

BLM: Stop at the BLM office at 345 E. Riverside Drive in St. George for maps and trip information. Office hours are 7:45 a.m.-5 p.m. Monday-Friday, and 9 a.m.-5 p.m. on Saturday, Mountain Time. Phone (435) 688-3200, azwww.az.blm.gov/asfo/index.htm.

Camping: Eleven primitive campsites are available at Toroweap, first come, first served, and will accommodate up to eight people or two cars per site. One group site is available by reservations; call (520) 638-7870. All sites include a picnic table and fire pit; bring your own wood and water. There is no fee. Backcountry camping is available by permit only, from the BLM office in St. George.

Grand Canyon National Park: Toroweap is in an undeveloped area of the North Rim in Grand Canyon National Park. No fee for entry or use is required. This is not a good place for children; there are no railings or fences, and the overlook has drop-offs of nearly 3,000 feet to the Colorado River.

Maps: The BLM's Arizona Strip field map is essential for getting to the trailhead. For detail on the Lava Falls hike use USGS 1:24,000 topographic for Vulcan's Throne. Both are available at the BLM office in St. George or at mapping.usgs.gov.

---

dered how long it would be before a helicopter came looking for me. Probably days, I decided, so I had no choice but to go on.

Back on my feet I headed up the lava-strewn hillside searching for shade. It was a good hour before I found a four-foot boulder to crouch under. It was shady but I needed to drop my head down in my lap, and it was terribly uncomfortable.

My watery Gatorade was running low now, and I tried in vain to find the next cached supply.

Every boulder looked the same now. I came to a steep ledge that I hadn't remembered, and didn't see any cairns to mark the trail. I had the choice of skirting a steep cliff on the left or climbing up onto the ledge. Neither looked safe and a fall from either path could have been fatal. I chose climbing up the ledge.

Finding the route now became easier, and the terrain itself less difficult, so I completed the next 500 feet in a daze, thirsty, hot, and exhausted, but pretty sure I would survive. I found the next Gatorade but left it for David, Laurie, and Phil knowing it was only about a half hour to the car where we had left an ice chest, packed with cold spring water. When I finally reached that water, I wouldn't have traded a pint of it for a case of vintage champagne.

I drove directly to the ranger station, but no one was there, so all I could do was leave a note. I spent the night alone at the campsite, worrying, and then packed up the car and waited till noon. If at least one of the others, or a ranger, didn't show up by then "Plan B" was to drive out to a phone, telephone the rangers to see if Phil had been picked up by a boat or helicopter, and start a rescue operation if necessary.

I was pouring the spare gasoline into the tank when I saw David and Laurie's Jeep Cherokee come down the slickrock road toward our campsite. They had a very weary looking Phil too, but he was all in one piece. The long hike had been rough on all three, but working together had brought them through. We celebrated by unpacking the car and spending another night in Toroweap with our two new friends, David and Laurie. We will remember them, with gratitude and fondness, as long as we live — which already may have been longer than if we hadn't met. ◆

Gary Ladd is a full-time nature photographer and author of Gary Ladd's Canyon Light: Lake Powell and the Grand Canyon, *published by Stephens Press.*

Blocks of Esplanade Sandstone teeter on the rim of Toroweap Overlook.

ON FOOT IN THE DESERT

{THE RARE OASES OF JOSHUA TREE NATIONAL PARK}

BEST KNOWN INTERNATIONALLY AS A ROCK CLIMBING MECCA with over 3,000 established routes, Joshua Tree National Park also has 191 miles of hiking trails, many of which lead to areas unexpected in a generally harsh desert environment. For instance, there are five lush palm oases in the park, all home to the California fan palm, *Washingtonia filifera*, the only palm tree native to western North America.

PHOTOGRAPHY BY MICHAEL CLARK

There are only 158 desert fan palm oases in North America. Fan palms require a constant supply of water; here, they get it because an earthquake fault allows underground water to reach the palm roots through fractures in the rock.

For most visitors who want to see one, the jumping-off place is the Oasis Visitor Center, in the northern area of the park near downtown Twentynine Palms, Calif. Here you can get information and maps, and take an interpretive tour of the Oasis of Mara, most popular of the five. The Serrano Indians who settled here gave it the name, said to mean "place of little springs and much grass." It's only a hundred yards from the visitor center a half-mile loop trail takes you into the palms and around the oasis.

Just a few miles away, and affording a

Elina Arenz-Smith hiking out to Headstone Rock near Ryan Campground.

Sunset paints rich colors on the Old Woman formation in Hidden Valley.

more private experience, is the Fortynine Palms Oasis. Cindy VonHalle, an interpretive ranger, told me, "The Fortynine Palms hike is one of the best in the park for the first time visitor, a beautiful pocket in the desert."

From the Fortynine Palms trailhead,

days. The palms live an average of 150 years and can grow as tall as 75 feet, making them the tallest North American palm species. Their fan-shaped leaves can be six feet long and nearly as wide. Indians used the fronds to build waterproof dwellings.

destroyed, the tree dies. In palm trees, however, the vascular system is dispersed through the trunk — an adaptation that makes them resistant to fire; in fact, fire is sometimes thought to benefit palms. Cahuilla Indians periodically torched some of the oases to stimulate

{ THE JOSHUA, YUCCA BREVIFOLIA, IS NOT REALLY A TREE BUT A LARGE MEMBER OF THE LILY FAMILY. }

the first half-mile brings you to the highest elevation of the hike, where you have views of the city of Twentynine Palms and your first glimpse of the oasis in the canyon below. Descending down the rocky trail, you'll find mesquite, brittlebush, and a large concentration of red barrel cactus.

This oasis is thriving and is home to a lot more than forty-nine palms these

ABOVE: The Fortynine Palms Desert Oasis in the northern section of Joshua Tree.

Bright green when living, these fronds die off gradually, forming a covering called the shag, skirt, or petticoat. Inside the shag live many desert creatures; the western yellow bat roosts only in palms. You might also see a hooded oriole, and the dime-sized holes in some older palms are made by larvae of a specialized beetle.

In hardwoods such as apple trees, the vascular system, which carries water and nutrients to the leaves, lies immediately under the bark; if the bark is

production of their edible fruit, and to remove sharp fronds from the oases' floors.

Three more oases are located an hour's drive away, in the southern area of the park, near the Cottonwood Visitor Center. The drive itself is worth the trip, for it takes you through the transition zone of the park's two deserts. The eastern part of the park is Colorado Desert, (an extension of the Sonoran Desert, with vegetation such as the ocotillo more usually associated

Joshua Tree is widely known for climbing opportunities but the hiking alone is worth the trip.

Getting there

Location: Joshua Tree National Park, Calif. about 212 miles from Las Vegas.

Directions to Oasis Visitor Center: From Las Vegas take U.S. 93/95 south for about 20 miles. At Railroad Pass, go right onto U.S. 95 south toward Searchlight and Needles, Calif. Drive about 79 miles and take Interstate 40 west. Drive about 17 miles and turn onto Route 66 west (a National Trails Highway). Drive 46.6 miles and go left onto Amboy Road for 46 more miles. Turn left onto Adobe Road for 2 miles to California Route 62, Twentynine Palms Highway. Turn left and drive a half-mile to the Oasis Visitor Center on your right.

Directions from the Oasis Visitor Center to the Cottonwood Visitor Center: Take Utah Trail south for 4 miles to the north entrance of the Park. Drive 4.8 miles and turn left onto Pinto Basin Road and drive for 32 miles to Cottonwood Visitor Center.

Season: October-April.

Oases Hikes

Oasis of Mara: Located at the Oasis Visitor Center

Length: Half-mile loop.

Trailhead elevation: 1960 feet.

Difficulty: Easy

Fortynine Palm Oasis: From the Oasis Visitor Center drive 4 miles west on California 62 to a left onto Canyon Road. Drive 2 miles to the road's end and trailhead.

Length: 3 miles round trip.

Trailhead elevation: 2,720 feet.

Elevation gain: 360 feet.

Elevation loss: 360 feet.

Difficulty: Moderate.

Lost Palm Oasis: From the Cottonwood Visitor Center drive 1.2 miles to the trailhead.

Length: 8.8 mile round trip,

longer to visit Munsen Canyon.

Trailhead elevation: 3,000 feet.

Elevation loss/gain: 590 feet.

Difficulty: Moderately strenuous.

Desert Queen Ranch: Admission is restricted to guided walking tours. Tours are a half-mile long, require about 90 minutes and are offered at 10 a.m. and 1 p.m. daily October through May. Summer tours are at 5:30 p.m. Wednesday and Friday. Fees are $5 adults, $2.50 for children under twelve. Located in Hidden Valley area. Reservations recommended, (760) 367-5555.

The Desert Institute: An educational field program of the Joshua Tree National Park Association offers courses in natural history, science, and the arts. (760) 367-5583, www.joshuatree.org.

Camping: Joshua Tree has nine campgrounds throughout the park, all open year-round with more than 500 sites available. For the hikes in this article, I would recommend Belle or White Tank campgrounds in the northern area of the park off Pinto Basin Road. They have no water and are first come, first served, but they are free. Cottonwood Campground in the southern end of the park has water, flush toilets, costs $10 per site per night, and is on a reservation

basis. All provide fire pits and tables. No wood gathering. Backcountry camping is allowed with a permit. (800) 365-2267.

Climbing: Motorized drilling is prohibited within park boundaries, and bolting is not allowed in designated wilderness areas.

Water: Potable water is available at the Oasis of Mara in Twentynine Palms, at Black Rock and Cottonwood Campgrounds, at west entrance, and at Indian Cove Ranger Station.

Ranger programs: Offered on the weekends from mid-October through mid-December and mid-February through May.

Joshua Tree National Park: Oasis Visitor Center, open all year except Christmas, 8 a.m. to 5 p.m. Cottonwood Visitor Center, open all year except Christmas, 8 a.m. to 4 p.m. For park information call (760) 367-5500, www.nps.gov/jotr.

Topographic maps: Trails Illustrated-Joshua Tree National Park 1:80,000. For more detail on the Fortynine Palms Oasis hike use USGS Queen Mountain 1:24,000. For more detail on the Lost Palms Oasis and Cottonwood Spring use USGS Cottonwood Spring-CA 1:24,000. Available at the Oasis Visitor Center or **mapping.usgs.gov**

12 miles

Arch Rock at sunrise. The formation is near White Tank Campground.

with Arizona) while the western part lies in the Mojave, where the most conspicuous life form is the Joshua tree.

The Joshua, *Yucca brevifolia*, is not really a tree but a large member of the lily family. The largest documented one in the park grows in the Queen Valley Forest and is about 40 feet tall. Although at one time it was thought to be as much as 900 years old, recent research puts its age at 200-400 years.

Two stops along the way, the Cholla Cactus Garden and the Sand Dune Nature Trails, are in the transition zone, and are geologically and botanically different from either desert.

Stopping at the Cholla Cactus Garden Trail is worth it; for the modest effort of hiking a quarter-mile loop, you'll be treated to the sight of a veritable forest of dense cholla. A few miles down the road, the sand dune area offers a self-

explanatory tour. VonHalle said, "This is a fun place to poke around looking for scat and tracks in the sand." It is common to see evidence of a variety of lizards, desert tortoises, and even kit fox here, she said.

To reach the final three oases, drive 1.2 miles south of the Cottonwood Visitor Center to the Lost Palm Oasis trailhead and Cottonwood Spring. Cottonwood Spring is but a few short steps from the

parking area. The Lost Palms Oasis hike will bring you to the largest fan palm stand in the entire park, and if you are willing to do some rock scrambling you can continue about a mile farther to Munsen Canyon, the fifth oasis and the least visited in the park.

These oases are just a small part of Joshua Tree National Park, which encompasses 794,000 acres, 585,000 of which are designated wilderness area.

Elevated to park status in 1994, the area has been under some form of federal protection since 1936, and has preserved cultural sites stretching 5,000 years from the prehistoric Pinto Culture through the era of ranching and mining that lasted into the 1940s. The latter two came together at the Desert Queen Ranch, which went broke as a mine site but was reclaimed as a ranch. Now the restored property provides an interest-

{ THE BEST PART OF JOSHUA TREE IS THE PART YOU'LL SEE WHEN YOU GET OUT OF THE CAR. }

ing glimpse into a place where life was hard but colorful.

The Park Service also has designated at least seven good back-road routes for high-clearance vehicles or bikes. But for my money, the best part of Joshua Tree is the part you'll see when you get out of the car and walk into the silent, lush, oases. ◆

Michael Clark is a freelance photographer specializing in outdoor adventure.

Jill Spivak in the Blue Grotto below Navajo Falls on the Havasupai Reservation.

FALLING WATER

Afoot in Havasu Canyon, where tires never tread

PHOTOGRAPHY BY KERRICK JAMES

A twenty-foot rope hung from a long sturdy branch of an imposing cottonwood tree above the clear, turquoise waters of Havasu Creek. My heart was beating rapidly as I stood perched on a large limestone-covered boulder. I gripped the rope, took a deep breath, and flew off swinging. I let out a great yelp, let go and dropped ten feet into the water. I went under, came up for air, grinning from ear to ear.

Hey, I'm not too old to swing from trees.

I must admit I was trying to keep up with my hiking partners, daughter Olivia, 17, and her friend Jason Reiman, 18, who are considerably less than half my age. We found the rope while hiking along Havasu Creek, Havasupai Indian Reservation's main drainage, which runs from the Coconino Plateau down to the Colorado River in the southwest corner of the Grand Canyon. We had come to visit Supai Village, see Navajo, Havasu, Mooney, and Beaver Falls, and do some hiking along the creek's travertine dams, pools, and verdant landscape.

We started our three-day trip the day before at the Hualapai Hilltop during an intense windstorm. From this plateau we hiked down about eight miles into Havasu Canyon and the village, and then another two to our campsite. The Havasupai Indian Nation has inhabited this area for over 700 years. Havasupai means people of the blue-green water.

There are no roads to the village and all travel, except for the occasional helicopter, is on foot or by horse or mule.

On entering the outskirts of Supai Village we found two natural stone pillars high on the end of a red mesa just before town. They are known as the Wigleeva and legend has it they are guardian spirits for the Havasupai. As long as they stand, it is believed, the tribe will occupy this land. The village is home to about 300 people. The streets are unpaved, lined with small wooden houses, each on its small plot of land. Most of the plots are fenced and some have small orchards of pomegranates, figs, and peach trees.

We found a store, post office, elementary school, restaurant, and helicopter pad arranged around the town square. A few locals hung out, and several mule trains walked through carrying supplies and bags. We checked in at the camping office, received our official backpack tags, and headed to the market to buy postcards. This was a must, since this is the last U.S. Post Office that uses mules to carry mail, and the postmarks take note of that fact. From there we headed under a huge cottonwood tree, over to the tribal cafe about twenty yards across the village square.

We ordered some cold drinks and Indian fry bread, then grabbed a seat by the window. We were only there for a few minutes when the lights flickered on and off, the wind gusted, and down the cottonwood came. This caused a flurry of excitement in the village, and I heard one local say she thought the tree to be more than eighty years old. For a small village this was a big event.

We headed out of town followed by two local dogs who would stick around for most of our trip. Both were medium-sized; one was brown and strong-looking, like a small bear, so Bear became his name. The other had short hair, mostly black with a little white. We called her Cookie because she looked like an Oreo.

About a mile-and-a-half out of town we noticed the seventy-five-foot Navajo Falls on our left. To get a good look at them we walked down a small spur trail to their base. Water flowed through a rich plant community of ferns and riparian plants down into pools of water, a secret paradise that is often overlooked by those heading to the larger Havasu and Mooney falls. A few minutes later the trail brought us near the one hundred-foot Havasu Falls. We couldn't wait to see them up close, but first we headed to the campground, found a site along the creek, and made camp. We then headed back to the falls. Olivia and I headed straight for the water while Jason went around to the right on a path to have a close, yet drier, experience.

The large pools below the falls were the blue color of the Caribbean, and a stark contrast to the maroon travertine cliffs. The water gets its unique color from the calcium carbonate in the water that hardens and forms the cream-colored travertine terraces, natural dams, and sculptured pools. When the sunlight reflects into the water it appears turquoise.

Over the next few days while hiking the

FALLING WATER

canyon, we would find the easiest way to make river crossings was along the edge of these dams. They are strong and hard, although you must play a balancing game against the swift water that tries to pull you down with it.

After our swim we headed back to camp to put on some warm clothes and have a hot meal. We were in the last days of October; darkness fell early, and so did we. The sound of the creek's swift flow of water lulled us into a peaceful sleep.

Early the next morning, we woke with a start when Cookie and Bear started barking wildly. Peeking out of the tent I watched them chase two wild horses away from our campsite.

After a quick, hot breakfast we threw on our daypacks and headed downstream, which is north on this stretch of the river. This afforded us a look at the rest of the mostly unoccupied campground that stretched three-quarters of a mile along the creek to the top of Mooney Falls, our next destination. At the overlook above these 200-foot falls, we ran into four hikers on holiday from France. We talked with them about this remarkable place. It was named for D.W. Mooney, a prospector who fell to his death trying to descend the falls in 1882. The French foursome had attempted to descend the steep route to the bottom but decided it was too dangerous, and contented themselves with the magnificent birds-eye view.

We remained eager to try it ourselves, though. After just a few short switchbacks, we found a trail that seemed to just end at the top of a dark tunnel. Here, steps carved in the limestone brought us down into the darkness, took a left turn, and opened up to a viewpoint. These tunnels are thought to be natural caves, improved by people who widened the openings for easier access and added other safety features.

After another short tunnel we arrived at the top of a seventy-five-foot cliff. Here there are chains fastened to the canyon wall by long bolts; we needed to hold onto the chains and use the bolts as footrests to descend safely. The route is slippery and dangerous even so, and we were grateful for a wooden ladder covering the last ten feet.

At the base of Mooney we unloaded our packs and headed to the water. Olivia made it almost to the falls before the water's force became so strong she almost got knocked down. We had the place to ourselves except for the hikers above, who were looking down at us and taking photos. We swam and took our own pictures. I remember thinking this had to be one of the most fabulous places on earth.

Feeling invigorated, we put on our packs

and headed farther downstream hoping to reach Beaver Falls, located some three miles distant. The route wasn't as well worn as those farther up the creek, and in places the trail was faint.

Although canyon grapevines (*Vitis arizonica*) grow all over Havasu Canyon, we came upon about a half-mile stretch where the vines completely dominate. They climbed the canyon walls, in some places forty feet high. Along the creek banks, they climbed the trees. We walked a narrow trail with the grapevines surrounding us waist high.

After our third river crossing, the trail led us high onto the right bank, headed downstream, and led us down a corkscrew passage to a giant palm tree — the only palm we saw in the canyon.

The path ended here, and there was nowhere to go but up. Here someone had left a climber's rope with footholds tied in it. Olivia and Jason made it up easily while I held the rope taut from the lower end, but nobody remained below to hold the rope for me, and I found it tricky climbing with the rope dancing around. Persistence finally prevailed, however. We walked about fifty yards farther and were looking down at Beaver Falls.

Beaver Falls are spectacular but not as grand as the other falls, and partially hidden from view by trees. Yet it was worth the journey to see the different character of this canyon downstream from Mooney Falls.

We took it slow on the way back to camp, exploring and checking out spur trails that brought us to old mining sites and to side canyons. This is also where we found the rope swing from which we all had a memorable ten-foot plunge. We took one more swim before making the steep ascent of Moody Falls, toward camp, a meal, and some rest. Leaving early the next morning, we found ourselves envious of the hikers we met, who still had most of this lovely trip in their future.

The hike out wasn't physically hard, just plain long. That last uphill mile was tiring. Olivia and Jason power hiked and made it back to the hilltop in two-and-a-half hours. They hadn't stopped the whole way. Since I took a few rests I arrived about thirty minutes later.

I still think a lot about my swing on the rope and wonder if it will be the last one I ever do. I hope not. For now, I'm not too old to play Tarzan. ◆

Kerrick James has photographed the West for more than twenty years. His work has appeared on more than sixty covers of magazines including Arizona Highways, Alaska, Cerca, Sky, *and* Sunset.

Waders play in Havasu Creek near Supai Village, Arizona.

Hikers descend the Cliff
Trail to Mooney Falls.

Getting there

Location: Havasu Canyon, on the Havasupai Indian Reservation in Grand Canyon, Arizona, about 218 miles from Las Vegas.

Directions: From Las Vegas, take U.S. 93 south about 100 miles to Kingman, Arizona. Go east on Interstate 40 for about 4 miles and take exit 53 onto Arizona Route 66 east. Drive about 54 miles to a left on Indian Route 18 (5 miles past Peach Springs and a paved road). Drive 60 miles north to Hualapai Hilltop parking area and trailhead.

Season: Year round, but March to May and September to November are best.

Length: Hualapai Hilltop to Supai Village, 8 miles one-way. Supai Village to campground, 2 miles one-way; Havasu and Mooney falls are on respective ends of the campground. Campground to Beaver Falls, about 3 miles one-way. Campground to Colorado River, about 8 miles one-way.

Approximate elevations: Hualapai Hilltop, 5,200 ft.; Supai Village, 3,200 ft.; Campground, 2,800 ft.; Beaver Falls, 2,300 ft.; Colorado River, 1,900 ft.

Difficulty: Moderate to Mooney Falls, then hazardous

Water: Havasu Creek has water year round, but you must treat it before drinking. Fern Spring, just off the main trail in the campground, has a permanent flow of water.

Equipment: Hiking boots, water shoes, or sandals; all should have treads that grip very well.

Hazards: Flash flood danger, cliff exposure. Dogs, ravens, and squirrels will try to get your food and trash.

Mules and horses: Pack mules are available. Weight limit is 130 pounds, in up to four packs or bags. Duffel bags are preferred. $75 each way. If you prefer to ride down, you can also rent a horse for another $75 each way. Reservations are required and prices are subject to change. (928) 448-2141.

Helicopter service: Service from Hualapai Hilltop to Supai Village. March 15-Oct. 15 runs Tuesday, Friday and Sunday; Oct. 15-March 15 runs Friday and Sunday, 10 a.m. to 1 p.m. Supai residents get priority; other seats are first come, first served. Air West Helicopter Service, (623) 516-2790.

Havasupai Indian Reservation: Alcohol and firearms are illegal on the reservation. Cash or Visa accepted for camping, entry permit, and lodge; café and market accept cash only. Prices may vary with season. Havasupai Tourist Enterprise, P.O. Box 10, Supai, Ariz. 86435. (928) 448-2928. For reservations start calling months ahead, because phone has been constantly busy or down. Or try **www.havasupaitribe.com**.

Permits: Entry fee $20 per person. Pick up your backpack tag at the campground office in the village.

Camping: The campsite is located about 2 miles from Supai Village. No campfires, but camp stoves are allowed. All trash must be packed out. Reservations needed. $10 per person per night. (928) 448-2141.

Lodging: Havasupai Lodge in Supai Village has 24 rooms with double beds, private baths, and air conditioning. No television or phone service. Reservations needed, at least six months in advance or longer for specific dates. (928) 448-2121.

Topographic Maps: National Geographic/Trails Illustrated-Grand Canyon National Park. For more detail, use U.S.G.S. Supai and Havasu Falls 1:24,000, available from **www.mytopo.com** or **mapping.usgs.gov**.

Services: Fill your gasoline tank in Kingman, Arizona, your last chance.

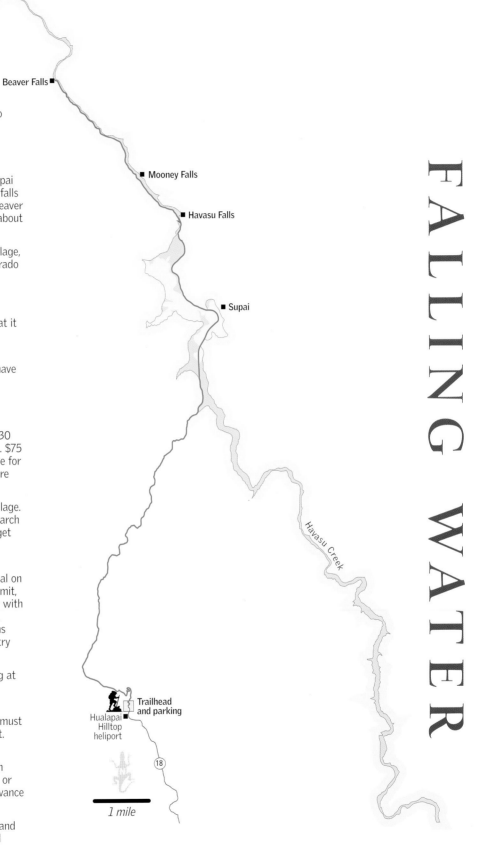

Beaver Falls ■

■ Mooney Falls

■ Havasu Falls

■ Supai

Havasu Creek

Trailhead and parking

Hualapai Hilltop heliport

18

1 mile

FALLING WATER

The hike ends at the saddle overlooking the Spring Mountain Ranch State Park; the Las Vegas Strip is visible in distance.

Rainbow Spring

Southern Paiutes picnicked in this fine and private place

Although Red Rock Canyon National Conservation Area is a well-known hiking area, not too many people have hiked its western escarpment. One great hike, although not an official one, is to Rainbow Spring. It takes a little more time to get to the trailhead than do some better-known paths, but once you do you will be rewarded with flowing water, Southern Paiute history, far-reaching panoramic views, and an overlook into seldom-seen Sandstone Canyon.

On my last visit I brought along two local hikers, neither of whom had ever before visited this part of Red Rock. From Lovell Canyon Road we drove three miles on a gravel road until boulders blocked our progress. We parked there, and this served as our trailhead. From here we followed a ribbon of water up the road to the partially dammed flow of Rainbow Spring.

The north part of the road is the official boundary of the Rainbow Mountain Wilderness Area, formally called and mapped as the Pine Creek Wilderness Study Area. The wilderness area is managed by the Bureau of Land Management and mostly within the Red Rock National Conservation Area.

We left exploring Rainbow Spring for later and continued up the road. With a bit of searching and using our topographic map we located Bootleg Spring, a much smaller water source, on our right.

The road soon forked and after going left about twenty yards we found an agave roasting pit on our right. This prehistoric kitchen was most likely used by the Southern Paiutes hundreds of years ago. Paiutes used such pits to slow-roast meats and vegetables. They especially took advantage of the Utah agave and the Mohave yucca plants that grow abundantly in this area. A fire was built in the pit and cobbles of limestone were heated in the fire; when the fire had burned down to coals, food was laid on the bed of coals and hot rock, then covered with vegetation and earth.

Because the limestone would eventually break down, the Indians raked out the fire-cracked rock to the sides of the pit and added new stones to the center. Through repeated use of the same pit, the discarded stones would create a ring suggesting a volcanic crater. We measured the pit from the outside edge of the used stones and found it to be an impressive sixty feet across. Signs at the site remind visitors that the Archaeological Resources Protection Act safeguards these remains of an Indian encampment.

As we walked up the road another twenty or so yards, a

PHOTOGRAPHY BY JIM K. DECKER

The author leads a group of visitors down the wash on return leg of the round trip.

large cairn marked our left turn off the road and onto a well-worn, but narrow, trail. We meandered along this for about five minutes until we arrived in a ten-foot-wide wash. On our left was a rock outcropping and below it a small cliff, then the continuation of the wash. We saw what we thought might be another roasting pit on the left bank about a hundred yards away, and decided to check it out on our return. Although a path could be seen heading up the hill across the wash, we turned right and headed up the wide gravel wash.

The walking was easy for the first quarter-mile and then it narrowed. In many spots we needed to walk along the bank to skirt boulders, logs, or trees. We continued up until a large branch blocked the path. Soon we found a cairn indicating the route turned right. Here a faint trail brought us up a steep incline and after about fifteen minutes we arrived at the saddle and overlook on top of Sandstone Canyon.

Here we were standing between Sandstone Mountain to the south and Indecision Peak to the north. We could see the Las Vegas Strip and as far away as Arizona.

One of the best views, though, was the birds-eye view into the 520-acre Spring Mountain Ranch State Park. It was green and lush-looking compared to the rest of the desert floor. A pair of binoculars afforded us a good look at the man-made reservoir built in the late 1940s to irrigate the pastures and provide water to the owners. It is still used today to water the grassy yard of the main house and the cattle still raised in the park, although water for human consumption now comes from a system fed by one of more than fifty springs on the ranch Lower Sandstone Canyon is only accessible to hikers by special tours arranged through Spring Mountain Ranch's interpretive ranger.

Although I have been told there are no Indian petroglyphs in the immediate vicinity, there are names inscribed in the walls by the early pioneers that came through here. Bighorn sheep and mountain lion also reside in this canyon. On our return we decided to stay in the wash the entire way back. When we arrived back at the rock outcropping, instead of going left and back on the footpath we headed down a four-foot dry fall and then a ten-foot cliff, aided by some natural footholds and handholds. This brought us back into the wide gravel wash. Another forty feet or so farther along, we found the second agave-roasting pit up a bank on our left, similar in size to the first one yet more oblong.

We continued down the wash about fifty yards until it joined a larger one. We went left and found ourselves at the upper end of Rainbow Spring. Here we found rushes, grasses, and a riparian habitat. There was also an old corral made from juniper logs and barbed wire.

This spring is home to one of two species of spring snails found nowhere in the world except the Spring Mountains. This one, whose scientific name is *Pyrgulopsis deaconi,* exists in only four springs. You probably won't catch a glimpse of one, though, because the snail is the size of a pinhead.

We backtracked a bit to skirt the spring and then walked along its bank past a few cascades and pools of water and then down next to the small man-made dams where we started.

As we were leaving, my guests thanked me for taking them to this special place. They were grateful that Southern Nevada offers so many places like Rainbow Spring, still little known, exciting to explore, yet close to home.◆

Jim K. Decker has been a photographer in Las Vegas for more than 20 years. He specializes in large-format photography of outdoor subjects.

A corral of juniper logs and barbed wire remains at Rainbow Spring.

Getting there

Location: Rainbow Spring, on the western escarpment of Red Rock Canyon National Conservation Area, about 37 miles west of Las Vegas.

Directions: From Las Vegas – take Interstate 15 south to Nevada Route 160, at the Blue Diamond exit. Drive 23.3 miles west to Lovell Canyon Road (National Forest Road 537). Go right for 0.9 miles, turn right onto National Forest Road 541, drive 3 miles and park.
From Red Rock Canyon's BLM Visitor Center – take State Route 159 south about 11 miles. Take a right (west) onto State Route 160. Drive about 13 miles west to Lovell Canyon Road (National Forest Road 537). Go right for 0.9 miles, turn right onto National Forest Road 541, drive 3 miles and park.

Season: October through May.

Length: 2.8 miles round trip.

Elevation at trailhead: 5,589 feet.

Elevation gain: 431 feet.

Difficulty: Moderate, but finding the route can be difficult.

Water: Although Rainbow Spring has a permanent supply of water, it is easier to bring your own. Using the spring might disturb the very rare snails that live there. If circumstances require using spring water, it's important to treat it before drinking.

Hazards: Rattlesnakes, flash flood danger in washes and on access road. Cliff exposure at Sandstone Canyon overlook.

Camping: No dispersed camping is allowed in the Red Rock Canyon National Conservation Area. The Red Rock Canyon Campground (formerly known as the 13-Mile campground) is 2 miles east of the BLM Visitor Center on West Charleston Boulevard (State Route 159). There are 71 individual campsites and five group sites. Fee is $10 per night per site.

Red Rock Canyon National Conservation Area: BLM

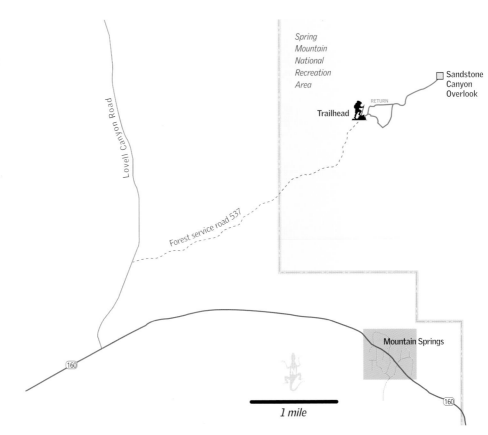

1 mile

Visitor Center, on Red Rock Canyon's scenic loop road, is open 8 a.m.-4:30 p.m. from November through March, and 8 a.m.-5:30 p.m. April through October. (702) 363-1921, **www.redrockcanyon.blm.gov.**

Spring Mountain Ranch: The main ranch house is open daily 10 a.m. - 4 p.m. Guided tours of the ranch and its historic sites are available daily. Special tours

of Sandstone Canyon may be arranged through the park's interpretive ranger. Nevada Division of State Parks, (702) 875-4141, **www.parks.nv.gov/smr.htm.**

Topographic maps: Toiyabe National Forest, Las Vegas Ranger District, 1:100,000. For more detail use USGS Mountain Springs and Blue Diamond 1:24,000. Available at the Red Rock Canyon Visitor Center or **mapping.usgs.gov/.**

HARROWING HIKING

HEAVENLY VIEWING

The challenging (and often scary) 2.5-mile journey to Angels Landing gives an unrivaled look at the beauty of Zion Canyon

LARRY ULRICH

Angels Landing is the prominent point in the right foreground, affording brave hikers a divine view of Zion Canyon below. This view is from Observation Point.

FRANK SERAFINI

The first part of the hike involves ascending switchbacks that begin near the Grotto Picnic Area.

One great thing about living in Las Vegas is its close proximity to some of the best hiking areas in the country. My two teenage daughters and I took advantage of this on a last-minute weekend getaway that brought us to Zion National Park, just a few hours away in southern Utah.

We weren't sure what hikes we would do, but a visit to the Zion Canyon Visitor Center changed that. I saw Whitney and Olivia eye a poster-sized photograph of the narrow sandstone switchbacks known as Walter's Wiggles, part of the trail to Angels Landing. They seemed eager to walk the Wiggles, so we had a plan in place for the next day.

Chains are in place for much of the final half-mile of the trail to help hikers up the steep terrain.

The next morning we hopped on the first shuttle bus from the visitor center. At 6:30 a.m., we were among a handful of early birds making the trip up Zion Canyon. It took about twenty minutes on the shuttle to reach our stop, at the Grotto Picnic Area. From here, we could see the prominent red sandstone monolith called Angels Landing, which rises about 1,500 feet above the canyon floor. It appeared inaccessible to anyone but technical climbers, and we wondered how the route would take us to the top.

We crossed over a wooden footbridge that brought us to the west bank of the North Fork of the Virgin River. Here we turned right, officially starting our hike.

FRANK SERAFINI

Zion Canyon and the Virgin River, as well as the start of the trail to Angels Landing, are visible after completing the first set of switchbacks.

This was the West Rim Trail, one of the first built in the park, and would lead us up to Angels Landing. The trail was paved and an easy, gentle ascent brought us up to the base of Zion Canyon's west wall. As we approached the canyon's edge, we finally arrived at steep zigzagged switchbacks cut into the wall that served as our route up and into Refrigerator Canyon.

This is a hanging canyon — a side canyon with its mouth lying high above the floor of the main canyon. In this case, it's about 500 feet above the floor. The temperature cooled dramatically in this canyon, and it was like a secret passageway. On our left was a boulder-filled gorge where white fir and bigtooth maple trees grew. To the right were sandstone walls with rock formations and caves that Whitney and Olivia couldn't resist exploring. We continued up the trail and came to Walter's Wiggles.

Walter Reusch, Zion's first acting superintendent, was the force behind this project, hence the name. This engineering feat was Reusch's answer to safely getting hikers up the 300-foot cliff to access the panoramic views on top. Back and forth we walked up the twenty-one short paved switchbacks cut into the steep rock, stopping only to take

One wrong step could be your last, for many areas have sheer drops of more than a thousand feet to the canyon floor.

photos and to converse briefly with two other hikers.

They were returning from the upper section of the West Rim Trail, and had just done the last harrowing part of Angels Landing. They asked us to take their photo. Each had a wide aluminum chair, the old-fashioned type with webbed seats, commonly seen at parades. These chairs don't fold very compactly, and looked pretty awkward for backpacking.

At Scout Lookout, there are fine views into Zion Canyon, and this marks the end of the trip for many. We had a decision to make here — call it a day or go the last one-half mile to the top of what we heard was a spine-tingling trail. We decided to go for it, and with Olivia leading we started up the uneven terrain along the ridge. Here, in many places, heavy chains are bolted into the rock to help hikers across the steep places. One wrong step could be your last, for many areas have sheer drops of more than a thousand feet to the canyon floor.

In one area, there are drops on both sides of a ridge barely five feet wide, with a narrow footpath in the middle. I thought about turning around but that seemed even more dangerous on this tricky footing, so on I went. I wondered how the backpackers we met maneuvered this terrain with those chairs on their backs.

With some effort and a few rests, we all made it safely to the summit, sharing it only with some weather-beaten pinyon pines that seem to grow straight out of the rock, contorted from years of wind and weather.

The panoramic views were the finest we had seen, even in a park where the awe-inspiring is commonplace. You can see miles down Zion Canyon, as well as north to the Temple of Sinawava. Within the lush green canyon floor was a small ribbon of water that was the Virgin River. It appeared small and insignificant at this height, contrasted against the immense sandstone walls surrounding the canyon. We stayed a while enjoying the view until other hikers started to arrive.

Going down was even more awkward, therefore more treacherous and scary. Now we had a clearer view of the drop-offs. Descending along the chains on the narrow route was trickier, too, as other hikers were starting to arrive, and we had to wait a few times to let folks pass.

Once we had passed the sheer drops, the rest of the descent was satisfying. We had achieved our goal of seeing Walter's Wiggles and made it to the top. We passed many more hikers who were making their way up, some giving us a hearty hello, others just a courteous nod, and some looking like they would rather be somewhere else.

The three of us, of course, with the scary part behind us, felt very brave and superior. ◆

Frank Serafini recently shared author's credit with writer Ruth K.A. Devlin in Desert Seasons, A Year In The Mojave, *a book published by Stephens Press. He teaches children's literature at the University of Nevada, Las Vegas.*

Larry Ulrich of Trinidad, California, spends six months a year traveling with his wife and frequent co-author, Donna. They have published some of the most widely admired books of nature photography.

Getting there

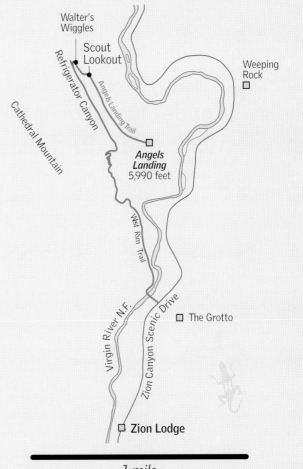

Location: Angels Landing, about 145 miles from Las Vegas in Zion National Park.

Directions: From Las Vegas, take Interstate 15 north 125 miles to Utah Route 9 (Exit 16 — Hurricane/Zion National Park). Follow Route 9 east for 19 miles to the east entrance of Zion National Park. Take shuttle to the Grotto Picnic Area.

Season: March through November.

Length: About 5 miles round trip.

Elevation at trailhead: 4,270 feet.

Elevation gain: 1,488 feet.

Difficulty: Moderate.

Hazards: Drop-offs and cliff exposure..

Camping: Watchman Campground is open all year for tent camping and RV hook-ups; for reservations call (800) 365-CAMP. South Campground is open April 1-October 31, has no hookups, and operates first-come, first-served. Information, (435) 772-3256.

Lodging: Only lodging in park is Zion Lodge, restored to its 1920s rustic design. Reservations strongly recommended. (888) 297-2757. For lodging in Springdale, Utah, and other nearby towns, contact Zion Visitors Bureau, (888) 518-7070, **www.zionpark.com/lodging.htm.**

Zion National Park: Entrance fee is $20 per auto, $10 for pedestrians, not to exceed $20 per family, good for seven days. From April to October, access to Zion Canyon is via shuttle buses, which run from early morning to late evening. Check schedules at the Zion Canyon Visitor Center. Information, (435) 772-3256 or **www.nps.gov.**

Zion Canyon Visitor Center: Located at the south entrance. Open 8 a.m.-7 p.m. daily, in summer. Shorter hours fall to spring.

Bicycling: The Pa'rus Trail offers a paved, car-free alternative for bicyclists to connect with the Zion Canyon Scenic Drive. Shuttle buses are equiped with bike racks.

Zion Human History Museum: Located one-half mile from the visitor center. Open daily 8 a.m.-5 p.m. Exhibits on Native Americans, pioneers, and park development. A 22-minute Zion orientation movie is shown hourly. (435) 772-3256.

Topographic maps: National Geographic-Trails Illustrated Zion National Park 1:37,700 feet. For more detail use USGS Temple of Sinawava (1:24,000) or BLM Kanab (1:100,000). Available at the Zion Canyon Visitor Center or **mapping.usgs.gov.**

Secret Stream

Water is plentiful on a winter journey in Red Rock Canyon

PHOTOGRAPHY BY JIM K. DECKER

The morning after a winter storm dropped a mix of snow and rain in the Red Rock Canyon National Conservation Area, a hiking buddy and I headed to the Calico Tanks Trail. This was a great time to visit because after a heavy rain, the trail transforms itself into a small stream and the depressions in the sandstone fill with water — a scene of unusual beauty in the desert.

Holes that hold water are called tanks, or *tinajas.* Some were small and partly frozen, the size of ice cubes, while others were large and pond-like. The trail is named for some of the largest, one of which always has water, making it a landmark in a dry country.

It was a holiday weekend and we had expected heavy visitor use, but nevertheless, we were surprised to see more than fifteen vehicles in the Sandstone Quarry parking area that served as our trailhead. We didn't let this deter us, because we figured some of the crowd would be dispersed on two other designated trails that leave from this area.

Most visitors, though, weren't even hiking. They were just making a nice outing of visiting the historic sandstone quarry site, seeing the agave-roasting pit, and exploring the Calico Hills walls and pockets near the parking area. It was obvious some hadn't even planned to get out of their vehicles, because we watched people ascending the hills in their street shoes, including a few who wore flip-flops and even heels.

Tinajas as large as this are rare in any desert country, and this one is essential to local wildlife.

Just a few hundred feet from the parking area, we stopped to visit the remnants of the Excelsior stone quarry that operated from 1905 to 1912. Ten-ton blocks were mined from the area's sandstone and hauled to Las Vegas by what was called the Big Devil Wagon. This was a steam tractor, so inefficient that it reportedly burned up to 400 gallons of crude oil a day. There are still many of the yellow sandstone blocks piled up, and old and young alike were scrambling around on top of them.

Backtracking about twenty feet or so from these quarry stones, we crossed a thirty-foot wide wash onto a well-worn trail, and headed right. We found a park service sign on the left that identified an agave-roasting pit, then a small sign directed us right on a spur trail for the Calico Tanks. The Calico Tanks trail immediately narrowed and headed down into another well-used trail that soon turned into a small wash surrounded by scrub oak, cat's claw, and manzanita.

Only ten minutes into the hike, small pools of water appeared, and patches of snow were found in the shadier spots. As we continued up the wash a bit farther, the bed became a small stream. At first we tried to avoid the water but eventually gave in to the certainty we were going to get wet. On some of the terraced sandstone we found small waterholes, and even small waterfalls trickling down. In some places they had frozen into icefalls.

Reeds rise through the upside-down reflection of the cliffs surrounding the Calico Tanks.

If you have the time, examine a few of the *tinajas* close up and you might see something that is usually overlooked — tadpole shrimp, *Longicaudatus*.

Within several hours of the rain, eggs that may have lain dormant for decades, in a dehydrated state, come to life after their hard shells are soaked in water. In their short lifecycle of only 20-40 days they grow to only an inch and a quarter. They are shaped like a horseshoe crab, and eat decomposing organisms such as leaves, insects, and animals.

With assistance from volunteers, the Bureau of Land Management has improved this trail so much in the past few years that it was a different experience than on previous visits. Route finding, which was an issue in the past, is now easy except in a few sections across the bare sandstone. Even there, if you just keep heading up the canyon, you won't get lost.

The tricky scrambling of the past has been eliminated with smooth sandstone steps, so well placed that some look like the work of a stonemason. The trail ends on a small rise, looking down about ten feet into the tank, and here we each found our own best route down. I took the direct route that had a natural slope and footholds. My buddy, taller than me, felt comfortable heading along the right sandstone cliff and making his way down from there. We measured the triangular-shaped

tank at 120 feet by 120 feet on the two shorter sides, making it an isosceles triangle. The middle was covered with a thin sheet of ice. This tank, the largest in the conservation area, is critical to the survival of the bighorn sheep and other wildlife.

This large *tinaja* marks the end of the trip for most, especially for those with children, but we decided to extend our journey by heading up a steep, twenty-foot sandstone cliff to the far end or southeast of the pool.

Our effort was rewarded with an unobstructed view of the visitor center and the first parking area in the Calico Hills. From here we climbed up about thirty more feet and had a view of the Strip and down into the private lands in Calico Basin. Above us on the towering sandstone cliff to our left we noticed a rock that looks like a sphinx that appeared to be watching over the valley below.

Like every good sphinx, this one had nothing to say, but such beauty requires little comment.◆

Jim K. Decker is a photographer for the Las Vegas Review-Journal. *Large-format landscape photography is one of his favorite art forms, and his work is frequently seen in* Cerca *publications.*

Getting there

Location: Calico Tanks, in Red Rock Canyon National Conservation Area, about 18 miles from Las Vegas.

Directions: From Las Vegas take Route 159 (Charleston Boulevard) west about 15 miles, and turn right into Red Rock Canyon's Scenic Loop Drive. The trailhead is at the Sandstone Quarry parking area, about 2.6 miles up the one-way loop.

Season: October through May.

Length: 2.5 miles round trip.

Elevation at trailhead: 4,350 feet

Elevation gain: 450 feet.

Difficulty: Moderate.

Hazards: Cliff exposure and some rock scrambling.

Camping: The Red Rock Canyon Campground (formerly known as the 13-mile campground) is off Charleston Boulevard 2 miles east of the scenic loop entrance. First come, first served, $10 per night, at 71 individual campsites and five group campsites.

Red Rock Canyon National Conservation Area: (702) 515-5350, www.redrockcanyon.blm.gov. Managed by the Bureau of Land Management. Guided hikes and programs: (702) 515-5367, www.redrockcanyonlv.org

Scenic Loop: The one way 13-mile drive is open 6 a.m.-8 p.m. April through September, 6 a.m.-5 p.m. November through February, and 6 a.m.-7 p.m. March and October.

Fees: $5 per vehicle per day; $20 buys a 12-month pass. There is no charge to visitors who walk or bicycle into the scenic loop.

BLM Visitor Center: Open 8 a.m.-4:30 p.m. November through March, and 8 a.m.-5:30 p.m. April through October. Located at entrance to scenic loop. (702) 515-5350.

Maps: Toiyabe National Forest, Las Vegas Ranger District, 1:100,000, the best topographic, is available at the visitor center. Red Rock Canyon hiking maps are free at center.

PHOTOGRAPHY BY MARK ANDREWS

Mid Hills to Hole-in-the-Wall

A full course of the East Mojave in a single hike

This butte lies along the trail near the lower end of the hike, before Hole-in-the-Wall.

U nlike some other units of the National Park System, the Mojave National Preserve wasn't created to showcase one unique feature, like the Grand Canyon or Yellowstone's unique geothermal activity. The idea here was to celebrate diversity; its borders encompass peaks rising to almost 8,000 feet on Clark Mountain and lands as low as 800 feet near Baker.

There are canyons, creeks, sand dunes, and forests. And surprisingly, I was able to sample much of this variety on one of only two trails yet established in the preserve: A hike from Mid Hills to Hole-in-the-Wall.

Eight miles long and mostly downhill, this trail started in a pinyon pine and juniper woodland, headed down into a fire-scarred valley, then into the open desert. Once I entered ghostly Banshee Canyon, I would need to climb 200 feet up and out through a fissure called Hole-in-the-Wall, using rings and pins to aid me.

Not just a stroll through the woods. Within the first half-mile of the hike I reached a ridge that put me at the highest elevation of the day, 5,600 feet. From there I had views of the New York Mountains to the north, Piute Range to the east, and Round Valley below.

Yet even that giant landscape was but a part of the 1.6-million-acre preserve, which stretches from California's eastern border 50 miles west, and from Interstate 15 some 40 miles south to Interstate 40. Historically a sparsely populated region of mining and cattle ranching, it became a preserve in 1994 with passage of the California Desert Protection Act. National preserves are managed by the Park Service and typically have all the characteristics of national parks, but Congress may permit hunting, trapping, grazing, and extraction of minerals or gas. In the Mohave Preserve, however, there are currently no active mines, and grazing is being phased out. Hunting is allowed in season, with a permit,

Barrel cactus and yucca flourish on cliffs of rhyolite, weathered into fanciful forms.

outside the wilderness areas that constitute about half the total acreage.

From the ridge, the path descended between two unnamed hills into Gold Valley, which was wide and had a more open landscape. A couple of miles into my journey, I arrived in a wide wash where signs point out two possible routes. You can go right and return to the trailhead via the gravel road, or go left via a large wash to continue to Hole-in-the-Wall.

The landscape is dramatically

These white cliffs rise up about 200 feet from the valley floor and stand out contrasted against the dark volcanic rock of the area.

different here. A lightning strike on July 12, 2002, touched off a fire that burned a couple of hundred acres before it could be controlled, and all that stands now are the black skeletal remains of juniper trees. It was hauntingly stunning. Mojave Preserve archeologist Dave Nichols said, "This used to be my favorite part of the hike, a thick pinyon-juniper forest."

Although the forest is gone for now, the fire did provide a good outcome for wildflower enthusiasts. In the spring of 2003 this area had one of the most spectacular displays of bloom in decades and with the good rains over the preceding winter, the spring of 2004 was expected to be just as showy. Nichols went on to say, "In late May and early June this area was carpeted with wildflowers; lupine, Indian paintbrush and other purple, yellow, and red wildflowers."

After a few hundred yards in the

wash, I found the brown metal trail marker sign on the right, alerting me to hike out of the wash and onto a footpath. The first time I took this hike I missed this important right turn and ended up following the wash east, then onto an animal path, and eventually out to the main road. It made for a pleasant backcountry hike, but I missed many of the highlights included in the designated trail.

The trail meandered southwest across the valley into another wash, then up an abandoned road to a massive rock outcropping, and past that to a ridge. Here I had my first views of Wild Horse Mesa, one of the largest in Southern California, and the Opalite Cliffs still a few miles away. These white cliffs rise up about 200 feet from the valley floor and stand out contrasted against the dark volcanic rock of the area. There is a prehistoric opal quarry under the cliffs. Nichols told me, "Native Americans busted off chunks and used this glassy stone to make scrapers, arrowheads, and other tools."

The sun was low in the sky as I neared the junction of Wild Horse Canyon and the short trail to Banshee Canyon and Hole-in-the-Wall, my final destination. The buckhorn cholla, barrel cactus, and the Mohave yuccas sparkled in the sun. I stood by one that was a lofty twenty feet tall. James Woosley, chief of interpretation for the preserve, said later, "These Mojave yuccas are the biggest I have ever seen in my life. Kind of freak yuccas." There are some near the trail, he added, that are 30 to 40 feet tall. Some in this region, in fact, are among the biggest in the world, and scientists are studying their growth patterns.

Next I entered Banshee Canyon. No

one can say for sure who named the canyon, but it is said that when the wind howls, eerie sounds suggest the mourning call of the banshee in Irish legends.

The canyon is magnificent and incomparable to anything I had ever seen before. Two-hundred-foot towering walls are composed of a crystallized form of lava known as rhyolite. Pocketed volcanic formations surrounded me on three sides, some bizarre and frightening looking, others human-like, suggesting another possible derivation of the canyon's name. The banshee was said to take three forms: a young woman, a stately matron, or a ragged old hag, and it takes but little imagination to see any of those forms among the oddly shaped rocks.

The canyon seems to be boxed in, but after following a well-worn path to the left, I found the entrance to the narrow chute that would bring me to what is commonly called the Rings Trail.

This final part of the hike was fun and easy. After a little rock scrambling, I reached places that were too steep to climb on my own, but there were rings and pins set into the rock to help me. The Bureau of Land Management installed these rings more than thirty years ago. At first it is awkward to use them, but I soon got the hang of it. Grab the highest ring you can reach, pull yourself up by your arms, and place your foot on a pin for support. Up I went into this passage until I reached the top and emerged at Hole-in-the-Wall, site of a picnic area, visitor center, and campground.

Hole-in-the-Wall supposedly received its picturesque name from Bob Hollimon, a minor cattleman who was just passing through about 1918, but changed his plans after receiving a surly greeting from cowboys of the huge 88 Ranch, which treated the officially public lands of the East Mojave as its private pasture. Bristling at the arrogance, Hollimon homesteaded 640 acres under the 88's nose, and became a professional annoyance.

Himself an able gunslinger, Hollimon never backed down from hired toughs and was more or less permanently under accusation of rustling 88-brand cattle. He always beat the rap, went home, and thought up ways to rub his victory in the 88's face.

It is in that context that Hollimon named this spot. It reminded him, he said, of a famous Wyoming location bearing the same name. In a livestock culture not many years removed from the Old West, the implication was clear to all. Everybody knew that the principal occupation, at the original Hole-in-the-Wall, was rustling. ◆

Photographer Mark Andrews is a frequent contributor to Cerca *publications. A photography program he produced for Las Vegas KLVX-TV, Channel 10, won an Emmy in 1999.*

LEFT: Lichens and moss colonize decomposed rhyolite.

TOP: The slot that helped inspire the name Hole-in-the-Wall. Ringbolts are to help hikers climb through.

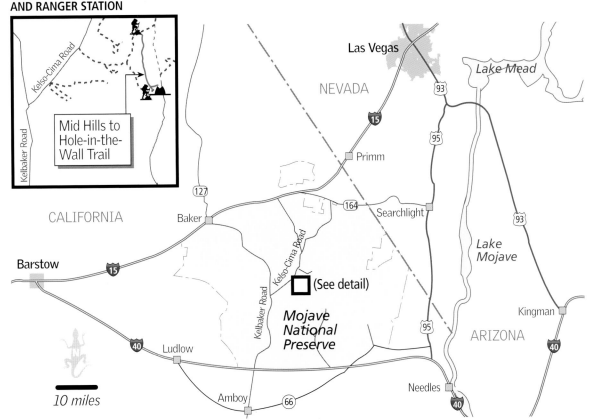

HOLE-IN-THE-WALL CAMPGROUND AND RANGER STATION

Mid Hills to Hole-in-the-Wall Trail

Kelso-Cima Road

Kelbaker Road

Las Vegas

NEVADA

Lake Mead

CALIFORNIA

Baker

Searchlight

Lake Mojave

Barstow

Kelso-Cima Road

Kelbaker Road

(See detail)

Mojave National Preserve

Kingman

ARIZONA

Ludlow

Needles

Amboy

10 miles

Getting there

Location: Mid Hills in Mojave National Preserve. Trailhead is about 88 miles from Las Vegas.

Directions: From Las Vegas, take Interstate 15 south about 51 miles. Exit onto Nipton Road and go east 4 miles. Take a right onto Ivanpah Road and drive 3.1 miles. Go right onto Morning Star Mine Road and travel about 22 miles. Go left onto Cedar Canyon Road for 5.8 miles. The road turns into gravel after 2 miles. Take a right onto Black Canyon Road for 3 miles. Go right onto Wild Horse Canyon Road and drive 2 miles to the signed trailhead on left, across from the entrance to Mid Hill Campground.

Directions to terminus: For this one-way hike you will need to have a vehicle waiting at the terminus. From the Mid Hills trailhead drive back to Black Canyon Road, go right, and drive about 7 miles, then take a right to the Hole-in-the-Wall Visitor Center and trailhead.

Season: October through May.

Length: 8.4 miles one-way.

Elevation at Mid Hills: 5,530 feet

Elevation at Hole-in-the-Wall: 4,265 feet

Elevation loss: 1,900 feet.

Elevation gain: 635 feet.

Difficulty: Moderate.

Water: Potable water is available at Mid Hills and Hole-in-the-Wall campgrounds.

Hazards: Rattlesnakes. Wear bright colors, preferably hunter's orange, when hiking during hunting season. For seasons, contact the California Department of Fish and Game, **www.dfg.ca.gov/.**

Services: There are no services in the Preserve. Gasoline is available in Primm and Searchlight, Nevada; Baker and Needles, Calif.

Camping: Mid Hills Campground has 26 sites and Hole-in-the-Wall Campground has 35 with fire rings, picnic tables, and a limited amount of potable water. Open year round, fee is $12 per night, first come, first served. Dispersed camping is allowed, except within one-quarter mile of water sources

Mojave National Preserve: No entrance fees. Open year-round. The Baker Desert Information Center is open from 9 a.m. to 5 p.m. daily, (760) 733-4040. The Needles Desert information Center is open from 8 a.m. to 4 p.m.; closed Mondays. (760) 326-6322. Ranger station at Hole-in-the-Wall, (760) 928-2575. Park Headquarters (760) 255-8800, **www.nps.gov/moja.**

Kelso Depot: Built by the Union Pacific Railroad in 1924, closed in 1985, scheduled to open again in late 2004 as a visitor center, museum, and bookstore.

Goffs Schoolhouse: Restored 1914 one-room school is centerpiece of a non-profit center devoted to history and culture of the East Mojave Desert. Hours change seasonally; consult **www.mdhca.org** or (760) 733-4482.

Topographic maps: National Geographic/Trails Illustrated-Mojave National Preserve 1:125,000. For more detail, use USGS topo Columbia Mountain, CA 1:24,000. Available at park information areas or **mapping.usgs.gov.**

Erosion from the orange and tan sediment of Cedar Breaks colors Ashdown Creek.

PLATEAU PLEASURE

From 10,640 feet, the trek is downhill most of the way

I t was just after 7 a.m. on a Sunday morning, over Labor Day weekend, when friends dropped me off at the Rattlesnake Creek Trailhead. Although it was August, the temperature was only in the forties. This wasn't surprising though, considering I was atop Southern Utah's Markagunt Plateau, at a lofty 10,640 feet.

I was embarking on my first solo hike of any length since I was a teenager, a day's journey that would bring me through extremely diverse mountain terrain. I would start off in a high alpine field, travel through densely wooded forests, cross flower-covered meadows, and two perennial streams, then pass through a magnificent limestone gorge complete with alcoves, arches, waterfalls, springs, and fossils. My route would be a steep one, descending some 3,600 feet over about ten miles.

I started my hike down an abandoned jeep trail; alongside a wood-and-metal fence in an open field at the northern boundary of Cedar Breaks National Monument. In just a few minutes, I came to a small wooden sign informing me I was entering the 7,000-acre Ashdown Gorge Wilderness Area. All but a small portion of my hike would fall within this wilderness.

The jeep trail soon became a narrow footpath that led me into a forest of Englemann spruce and subalpine fir. Unfortunately, the spruces have taken a beating since the mid-nineties from the

bark beetle epidemic, and many trees now stand as rusty colored skeletons. With so much dry fuel available here, fire is a hazard most of the time, so fire restrictions are in force much of the year.

The forest smelled woodsy and rich, thanks to the pines, spruce, and moist soil beneath my feet. I even found a bounce in my step from the cushiony soil, not usually encountered on trails in the Southwest.

Two spur trails within the first mile brought me to overlooks of the north side of Cedar Breaks, and these seldom-seen views were worth the few side trips, which took only a few minutes each.

Back on the main trail, the path descended sharply through stands of quaking aspen and conifers, including some scattered bristlecone pines. Although bristlecones are more concentrated in other areas of the wilderness, the few thriving here were an inspiration to me. Some still stood healthy and robust, although most were likely thousands of years old.

I didn't see any footprints on the trail, but I did find fresh hoof marks. I wondered if I would run into horse and rider later.

This trail has obviously been here for years, and I even found one aspen carved with a 1938 date. The forest gave way to a steep grassy hillside, where some overly enthusiastic group or individual had built cairns about four feet tall to mark the switchbacks. Then the route brought

PHOTOGRAPHY BY LIN ALDER

Hikers make their way by a cliff undermined by relentless erosion.

me under a full canopy of conifers, where the area beneath was dark, damp, and filled with colorful toadstools and mushrooms. It reminded me of some fairy tale from my childhood, in which mountain lions, bears — or worse — lurked in the shadows, stalking me, ready to pounce at any moment.

I left my paranoia behind when the trail broke out of the woods into a broad open meadow called Stud Flat. Here I took a break to soak up the sun, study the map, and get my bearings. Although peak wildflower season here is in July, there was still an incredible profusion of flowering asters, paintbrush, and daisies.

I believe Father Time does not deduct from our allotted lifespan the hours spent basking in meadows; unfortunately, I still had a schedule to meet, and was soon walking through

another wood. The terrain became increasingly steeper and a series of switchbacks helped me descend the canyon to gently flowing Rattlesnake Creek. I could still see the hoof prints in the soil, and I was impressed by the horse's ability to maneuver safely down this narrow path.

The route forded the river and continued high on the right bank, paralleling the stream's course. Many areas of the trail had been washed out, and in some places I had to jump a few feet across a gap.

I also found a nice stand of mature ponderosa pines here, some soaring a hundred feet or so, one at least four feet in diameter. One hadn't fared so well, probably a victim of lightning, and lay prone across the trail, blocking further progress. I climbed over it, careful to avoid its sharp broken limbs.

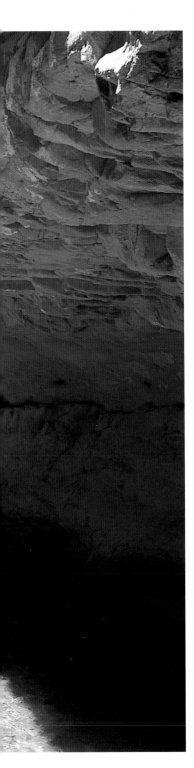

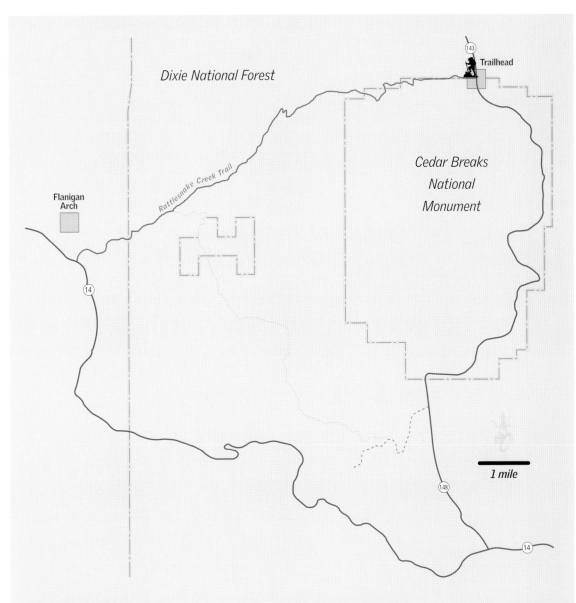

Dixie National Forest

Flanigan Arch

Rattlesnake Creek Trail

Cedar Breaks National Monument

Trailhead

143

14

148

14

1 mile

Getting there

Location: Rattlesnake Creek and Ashdown Gorge, about 190 miles from Las Vegas at northern boundary of Cedar Breaks National Monument.

Directions to trailhead: From Las Vegas, take Interstate 15 north 162 miles to exit 57, Cedar City, Utah. Go north on Utah Route 14, taking a right after 2 miles, which continues Route 14. Drive 15.4 miles and go left onto Scenic Byway 148. Drive 8.2 miles farther, (during which the road will become Utah Route 143 after you pass the turnoff to Panguitch), and look for the signed trailhead on the left, at the northern boundary of the national monument.

Directions to terminus: The hike ends at the confluence of Ashdown and Cold Creeks, 8 miles east of Cedar City on Route 14 in Cedar Canyon. Arrange to have a vehicle waiting at the parking lot just below Mile Marker 8 on the north side of the highway. Hiker will find an obvious jeep trail leading from the streambed about 50 yards up to the parking lot.

Water: Rattlesnake and Ashdown Creeks are perennial streams. A few springs can be found the last 2 miles of the hike. Always treat water before drinking.

Season: June to early October.

Length: 9.5-mile through-hike.

Elevation at trailhead: 10,460 feet.

Elevation loss: 3,600 feet.

Elevation gain: 160 feet.

Difficulty: Moderate.

Equipment: Sturdy walking staff. Boots appropriate for hiking and walking through water and on slippery rocks.

Hazards: Steep terrain, on primitive trail. High altitude may cause shortness of breath and fatigue. Flash flood danger in Ashdown Gorge.

Camping: Cedar Breaks National Monument has a 30-site campground with restrooms, water, fire pits, and picnic tables, at $12 per site, first come, first served. Open from June to mid-September. Dispersed camping is allowed in the adjacent Dixie National Forest, where fire restrictions are common, but there's no fee except for groups over 25.

Cedar Breaks National Monument: Open late May to mid-October. Visitor Center open 8 a.m.-6 p.m. Geology programs and nature tours. (435) 586-9451, **www.nps.gov/cebr**.

Jurisdiction: Ashdown Gorge Wilderness Area is maintained by the Dixie National Forest, headquartered at 1789 N. Wedgewood, Cedar City, Utah, (435) 865-3700, **www.fs.fed.us/dxnf/**.

Maps: National Geographic/Trails Illustrated, Cedar Mountain-Pine Valley Mountain 1: 75,000. For more detail use USGS Flanigan Arch and Brian Head 1:24,000. Available from **mapping.usgs.gov** or from Dixie National Forest Headquarters.

Although this was easy for a hiker, I knew the horse and rider would need to turn around here. On the other side I looked around and found the trail void of any hoof prints, and figured I had seen the last trace of them.

I couldn't have been more surprised when, downstream a quarter mile, I found more hoof prints. The horse and rider must have turned around at the log, headed back down the trail, dropped into the creek, traveled downstream, then back up to the trail. They constituted one very determined pair, and I felt comfort they were still with me, if only in spirit. When I reached the junction with the High Mountain Trail that comes in from the north, by Sugarloaf Mountain, I noticed the hoof prints heading up that trail. I was sorry

aplenty marked the stream's banks. Each bend in the creek created new anticipation as it cut its serpentine way between 500-foot walls.

Although it's possible for a hiker to skirt many of the bends by trails along the creek banks, I chose to walk in the streambed. I was rewarded for my damp decision with extra sights of natural beauty. I found a lovely cascade that dropped into a pool of water from a ten-foot waterfall. I needed to do some scrambling down boulders, but it just added to the excitement of the day.

The colorful walls of pinks and orange gave way to hues of tan and brown, and I found hundreds of areas where water seeped from the canyon walls, creating havens for

Because Ashdown Creek is the main drainage for Cedar Breaks National Monument, it is prone to flash floods, making the gorge an extremely dangerous place to be during heavy rain.

to lose the unseen partners who had already encouraged me through half the trip.

My own route led back to the streambed, where I sat awhile on the relative comfort of a large log, alongside a pleasing five-foot waterfall. I crossed the creek and headed to the only uphill section of the hike, which would bring me over the unnamed ridge that separates Rattlesnake and Ashdown Creeks.

After twenty minutes or so I started to catch glimpses of high canyon walls, and I realized I was now walking above the cliffs that formed Ashdown Gorge. Here I found an abundance of fossilized oysters imbedded in the rocks.

I could see the pink-and-orange banks of Ashdown Creek from here, but it was far below me and I could not imagine how the trail would take me down into the gorge. The creek is named after George Ashdown, an early settler and rancher who operated two sawmills. Remains of one of them can still be found about half a mile upstream from here.

The trail headed east for a short period, and after a steep descent I arrived in Ashdown Creek just above the gorge. Because this creek is the main drainage for Cedar Breaks National Monument, it is prone to flash floods, making the gorge an extremely dangerous place to be during heavy rain.

Confident because I had not only read the forecast but also checked the skies myself and found no signs of rain by either method, I headed downstream. The canyon walls immediately narrowed and I was now officially in Ashdown Gorge.

The gorge is predominately limestone, and along its banks were boulders and tree stumps, all covered with a layer of Limestone like a two-inch covering of pink snow. I found no evidence of man, but mountain lion and bobcat tracks

water-loving plants and wildlife. These seeps and springs create a hazard to the hiker, and for over a mile the innocent-looking streambed swallowed me up to my knees. This muck is made up mostly of clay mixed with subsurface water, and the combination acts like quicksand.

I started to see familiar landmarks, and knew I was getting to the last few miles of my journey and nearing Flanigan's Arch. Discovered in 1916 by William Flanigan, the flat-topped arch spans about fifty feet, is about 100 feet high, and about thirteen feet wide and thick. It is also very hard to find, and an even bigger task to climb. Since 1965, when the Sierra Club placed a log on the north end of the arch, about 400 people have completed the trip — only about ten a year.

The Forest Service has attempted to place signs by the creek to guide people in finding the arch, but they seem to disappear even when bolted onto rocks. The easiest way to locate it is to use the Flanigan Arch 1:24,000 topographic map, which has the arch marked. That will get you to the general area, then, as you head downstream, stay on the left bank and look for two major pinnacles about 500 feet up the canyon walls. Flanigan's Arch is just behind them.

From Flanigan's Arch downstream, I traveled at a slower pace, in no hurry to get back to the bustle of civilization. I was surprised and fortunate that even on a Labor Day weekend, and except for a determined horse and rider, I had this magic trail to myself.◆

Lin Alder of Springdale, Utah, specializes in outdoor subjects. His work has appeared in Backpacker, National Geographic Adventure, The New York Times, Outside, *and many other publications*

You can walk on dry land, but you'll miss some of the best parts, and most hikers elect to get wet.

Spirit Mountain

Hiking the holy ground of the Colorado River

It took thirty minutes of difficult rock scrambling before two friends and I made it to the first ridge and one of the few flat areas on the way up Spirit Mountain. We were hiking the highest peak in the Newberry Mountains, and one of extraordinary spiritual significance to the native peoples of this region.

Steep terrain and the lack of a well-defined route made this a strenuous hike, and we were happy to find a level area to catch our breath, take in the views, and consult the topographic map. We had discussed a few possible ways to reach Spirit's summit, but after studying the map, we had decided to start on the eastern side of the mountain, just off Christmas Tree Pass Road. We thought this was the easiest and safest route, but those are relative terms.

It had more elevation gain than some routes, and would take us up four different slopes, two of them extremely strenuous and steep with a lot of scrambling.

From the vehicle pullout where we parked, we walked up an old road, on which dead yuccas had been anchored with jute netting to discourage vehicle traffic and encourage the re-growth of vegetation. As soon as the road ended, we had to pick our route, for there was no obvious path. Going around the base of a rock outcropping on our left, we started uphill.

Spirit Mountain in sunset light, with pinyon pine.

PHOTOGRAPHY BY BRUCE GRIFFIN

Spirit Mountain

This steep terrain was full of boulders and cacti, so each of us took a different route according to what appeared the easiest.

About halfway up, a glint of white caught my eye, contrasting with the brown and tan rock hillside. It turned out to be a projectile point — a thin, flat, well-made blade about two inches long and an inch wide. The point was still intact but the flaked stone edges were no longer sharp, making me suspect they were dulled by decades or even centuries of drifting downhill in the gravel slope.

It was the third arrowhead I had found hiking over six months. I always consider finding one a good omen, suggesting the trip is going to go really well. As always, I left the point where I found it, and continued hiking, wondering who had worked this stone and how long ago.

Many white people call this mountain Newberry Peak, or Dead Mountain, but the Mohave people call it Avikwame, and the Hualapai, Wikame. All the Yuman-speaking people of the lower Colorado region consider it sacred ground, for they believe the mountain is the spiritual birthplace of their tribes.

It was here that the god Mastamho led the people, from their place of creation far to the west; here that he created daylight, sun, and moon. Here he divided the people into tribes — the Hualapai, Yavapai, Chemehuevi, Quechan, Kwaaymii, and Mohave. Then he sent off five tribes to inhabit the lands to both sides of the Colorado, but told the sixth, the Mohave, to build their houses nearby. When his work was complete, he turned himself into a fish eagle — an osprey — and flew away.

In 1998, the Bureau of Land Management and the National Park Service helped the tribes get the peak and the nearby canyons listed on the National Register of Historic Places as a traditional cultural property. Although the rules a hiker is expected to obey here are the leave-no-trace procedures of the National Park Service, those rules

Curiously, petroglyphs are not found on the sacred mountain itself, but Grapevine Canyon, near its foot, is a site especially rich in the ancient rock carvings.

seem particularly appropriate in a place regarded with reverence by at least six cultures.

Resting on the ridge, we enjoyed the first good views of the day — down into Lake Mojave, including part of Davis Dam, Laughlin, Bullhead City, and the range to our east, the Black Mountains of Arizona.

Resuming our uphill hike, we came to the most treacherous part of our trip. Large boulders, cliffs, and ledges on an extremely steep slope were our obstacles. At the top of this ridge was a sheer fifty-foot drop-off, so we backtracked about forty feet and headed to the right, or north. Now the ridge took

us through some fairly flat terrain where we could walk upright, providing a welcome break from the rock scrambling.

The next slope was shorter than the two previous, and we were getting closer to the top. We found a green metal pole, which we hoped indicated the summit, but we quickly realized our work wasn't over.

Here we were treated to our first views to the west and the final peak area to the north. There were two peaks above us, separated by a saddle. The one to the left, or west, was highest, although that wasn't obvious from here.

Walking north along the ridge, we found it well marked by cairns, and there was even a faint path. An open area down to the right of this ridge caught our eye and on inspection, we found it cleared of trees and brush to the eastern rim. As we walked down we found a hole about eight inches wide with bright green moss growing around it that was very damp, which we assumed was a old prospector hole that catches water. Below us, the mountainside was cleared of all vegetation from an area about thirty yards long and twenty yards wide. We inspected it more closely and found a large ring of rocks, about thirty feet across. Behind that were a fire pit and what appeared to be the marks of helicopter landing skids. It was an odd find, and I have been able to obtain no explanation for it.

We returned to the ridge and after a steady elevation gain we reached the saddle that separated the two small peaks. We headed left to a horizontal rock outcropping that we went over by finding a break in the cliffs. This led us to the top of a steep, narrow chute that we climbed down to reach the base of the final thirty-yard ascent to the summit. Those last few yards were steep but not tough, and we finally reached the old wooden survey post that marked the very top.

This could be the best panoramic view in Southern Nevada, and on a clear day like today, we could see more than a hundred miles. Just below us to the west were Paiute Valley, the community of Cal-Nev-Ari, and, beyond that, the mountain ranges of the Mojave National Preserve. Spread out to the east, some 3,000 feet below us, was Lake Mojave; we could see water flowing south from Cottonwood Cove. To the north we could see Searchlight and all the way to the peak of Mt. Charleston, some ninety miles away as the crow flies. Laughlin and Bullhead City were to our southeast and we could see the Colorado River as it serpentined south toward Needles and beyond. We realized we were looking at mountain ranges in four different states — Nevada, California, Arizona, and Utah.

As on many peak hikes, an army-surplus metal ammunition box contained the climbers' logbook, in this case three pocket-sized notebooks, two already full and the third half full. There was also a plastic bag full of business cards.

The mountaintop is very rocky and

Getting there

Location: Spirit Mountain, in southeastern Nevada, about 80 miles from Las Vegas.

Directions: From Las Vegas, take U.S. 95/93 south for about 20 miles. After climbing out of the Las Vegas Valley into Railroad Pass, go right onto U.S. 95 south for 49.8 miles, passing through Searchlight. Go left on Christmas Tree Pass Road and drive 10.2 miles to the parking pullout on left that serves as the trailhead.

Season: October to March.

Length: About 4 miles round-trip.

Elevation at trailhead: 3,360 feet.

Elevation gain: 2,280 feet.

Difficulty: Strenuous.

Water: Bring your own.

Special equipment: Gloves.

Hazards: Loose boulders, cliff exposure, route finding, and rattlesnakes.

Jurisdiction: Lake Mead National Recreation Area. Visitor information (702) 293-8907, **www.nps.gov/lame.**

Topographic maps: Trails Illustrated-Lake Mead National Recreation Area, 1:145,728. Available at Alan Bible Visitor Center or **www.trailsillustrated.com.** For more detail use USGS Spirit Mountain 1:24,000, available at **mapping.usgs.gov.**

1 mile

very small, with sharp drops on all sides, so wandering around isn't for the careless or the faint of heart. We spent about thirty minutes up top having lunch, reading the log entries, and writing our own.

On our way back down we took time to explore other possible routes for our next visit, but each proved too steep for a safe descent without rope. We realized the route we chose coming up was pretty darn good, and used it again going down. And though getting up the slopes had been strenuous, going down was even more difficult. In many of the steep areas we had to remove our packs, because they would have thrown us off balance. Cacti that we somehow avoided on the way up become a problem, and we all had to remove a few needles.

Whites are sometimes surprised to learn that despite Spirit Mountain's importance to many Native Americans, no petroglyphs have been found on it.

Archaeologists theorize that even though at least some of these rock carvings are also thought to have religious significance, Spirit Mountain may have been too sacred for such treatment. But two canyons over and a few miles away is Grapevine Canyon, one of Southern Nevada's largest petroglyph sites, which should be part of the itinerary for anyone's excursion to Spirit Mountain. A short and easy hike from the parking area takes you into the canyon where a spring, a few rock shelters, and impressive petroglyph panels can be seen.

Here, it is said, shamans of the six peoples came to seek the vision from which they derived their powers. Every shaman dreamed the same thing. In the dream, each stood in the house of Mastamho, atop the mountain Wikame at the beginning of time, and witnessed the waking of the world.◆

Bruce Griffin is a nature photographer headquartered in Tucson. He is a frequent visitor to the Spirit Mountain/Grapevine Canyon area.

SPRING MOUNTAIN SOLITUDE

POPULAR IN SUMMER, TRAIL TO MARY JANE FALLS IS UNCROWDED IN OFF-SEASON

When it comes to finding and enjoying natural waterfalls, the Las Vegas area doesn't offer many opportunities. But just an hour's drive away in Kyle Canyon in the Spring Mountains National Recreation Area, there are a handful of falls to see. The tallest and most impressive displays are the two that make up Mary Jane Falls. Although most of the water comes from springs high up on the limestone canyon walls, during the snowmelt they can be even more dramatic.

On a previous visit here in late spring I found the falls area a little too crowded, so on this trip I opted to go off-season. It was late November, and I had the place to myself as I walked along the boulder-lined gravel trail from the trailhead. The Mary Jane Campground was located here until it was washed out by a flash flood in the 1980s. It was never rebuilt because its location next to a large wash suggested the flood would repeat itself.

The falls were named after Mary Jane Griffith, who was the daughter of Robert Griffith and granddaughter of E.W. Griffith, Las Vegas founding fathers and developers of the original community here in Kyle Canyon. In

1914 E. W. constructed a sawmill and a log cabin here, just west of what is now the elementary school in Old Town.

Just a few minutes into the trail I found myself in a forest of ponderosa pines, white fir, aspens, and mountain mahogany. The aspens had already lost their golden leaves and the upper reaches of the canyon already had snow. Although common thistle, elderberry, willow, and other common plants are found here, some other species grow here and nowhere else. One, the rough angelica (*Angelica scabrida*), grows along the lower trail in the wash and in the avalanche chutes in the canyon. The Southern Paiutes, who occupied this area for more than a thousand years, brewed the roots, making a tea to soothe stomach aches and for chest and kidney disorders.

A gradual incline brought me deeper into the wooded canyon and then to the first of twelve switchbacks. A fallen thirty-foot ponderosa blocked a section of the second switchback but it was not a problem to skirt the tree. Although the trail is just a mile-and-a-half it has a steady elevation gain and can be strenuous, especially if you normally live some five thousand feet lower, in someplace like Las Vegas, and are unaccustomed to the thin alpine air.

Because of the trail's popularity, steep grade, and the harsh winter weather, it needs constant monitoring. In the past, people have made shortcuts across the switchbacks and caused plenty of damage to the plants and soil. The U.S. Forest Service works with the Spring Mountain Youth Camp forestry program to maintain and repair this route and some fifty more miles of designated hiking trails in the Spring Mountains Recreation Area. This very successful joint effort is in its thirty-second year, and the longest-running program of its type in the United States. Here they have placed jute netting, along with logs and tree branches, to rehabilitate the steep slope.

On the final switchback, flat rocks have been placed to make traveling easier along the base of the cliffs. Determined plants grow out of rock crevices in seemingly impossible areas,

A photographer can get behind the curtain of falling water at Mary Jane Falls and see others exploring the area.

(BY JIM DECKER)

and rock spires hang onto the cliff walls. The trees on this slope have taken on odd shapes from the wind, snow, and ice. I even found three trees that had started off as separate plants, and had grown into one.

Toward the end of the final switchback I passed a dry fall that was sculptured smooth from water, then soon after, I heard the active falls. The first waterfall is the grandest; unable to measure it, I estimated its height to be more than one hundred feet.

Water poured from its terraced face down to a thick base of ice and snow. I crossed the ice carefully and headed to the base of a wide ledge and overhang. Then I climbed up the ledge, using the natural footholds and handholds. Looking in, I could see icicles hanging from the ceiling and mosses and lichen growing within the overhang. The Forest Service discourages actually entering the overhang, because doing so would disturb fragile plant life, but you can see it all without going in.

Back below the ledge, I walked to its far side and found another waterfall and then a spur path that led to another, smaller overhang.

I did see a few chipmunks scurrying around that I presumed to be Palmer's, a species unique to the Spring Mountains. They are usually found at about eight thousand feet elevation, where the dominant vegetation is ponderosa, as on this trail. The Panamint chipmunk prefers a habitat just down the canyon, where mountain mahogany is more abundant. Although a close cousin, the Panamint chipmunk is found over a much wider range. It is difficult to tell the difference unless they are standing side by side, where the Palmer's chipmunk would be a little larger and a brighter color.

Returning to the falls, I gave another look to the top and watched the continual narrow flow of water drop onto the ice below. There is some run-off below that forms a small creek but quickly disappears underground after a hundred feet or so.

Although their appearance was not so grand as in the springtime, I appreciated the falls even more this autumn day, because I had them all to myself.

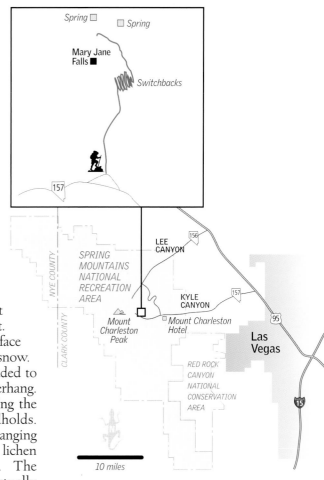

Getting there

Location: Mary Jane Falls in Kyle Canyon, about 38 miles from Las Vegas in Spring Mountains National Recreation Area and Humboldt-Toiyabe National Forest.

Directions: From Las Vegas, take U.S. 95 north about 17 miles. Go left on Highway 157. Drive 20.5 miles, go right on Echo Road. Drive .4 miles then left on gravel road for .3 miles to trailhead.

Season: Spring through fall. Snow in winter. Length: 1.5 miles one-way.

Elevation at trailhead: 7,840 ft.

Elevation gain: 1,040 ft.

Difficulty: Moderate.

Water: Carry water with you; falls are unreliable.

Hazards: Wet and slippery footing near falls in all seasons; cooler weather brings falling ice. Avoid contact with any wild animals.

Fire restrictions: Restrictions are common; watch for fire warnings.

Fees: None.

Camping: Fletcher View Campground has 12 sites at $19 per night, first come, first served. Kyle Canyon Campground has 25 sites, 15 available by reservation, $12 per night. Both are open from mid-May through mid-October and are located on Highway 157, a few miles before the trailhead. (702) 515-5400, www.reserveusa.com.

Jurisdiction: Humboldt-Toiyabe National Forest, Spring Mountains National Recreation Area, Las Vegas Ranger District, (702) 515-5400, www.fs.fed.us/htnf/smnra.

Topographic Maps: Toiyabe National Forest, Las Vegas Ranger District, US Forest Service. For more detail use Charleston Peak, Nevada 1:24,000. Available at the SMNRA Office, 4701 N. Torrey Pines, Las Vegas. (702) 515-5000.

IN HOT WATER

Where rock walls weep wax and stars shine in the daytime

It's the hiking I like; the hot springs are just the gravy." These are the words of Mike Henry, who I met this past January, simmering in the Arizona Hot Springs, along the Colorado River a few miles below Hoover Dam. Henry has been coming to the hot springs for about three years and could possibly be their most frequent visitor. Retired and in his mid fifties, he tries, during the cooler months, to visit as often as three times a week. When I talked to him he had also done the 5.6-mile round trip hike the day before, but here he was again. Suffice it to say he's familiar with the place.

On my way down I had taken the National Park Service's designated White Rock Canyon trail, a signed and easy-to-follow route that started along a ridge, brought me down into a wide wash and then into the canyon of volcanic rock and ash. The trail was a mix of sand and gravel, and was a little like walking on a sandy beach, but easier on the calves.

Within most of the canyon, the wash was about twenty to thirty feet wide although in some places only ten feet. It just kept winding along between the canyon walls and headed down toward the Colorado River channel, which is called Black Canyon here below Hoover Dam.

When I reached the river, the water was as clear and transparent as the Caribbean. Since it was January, I wasn't surprised that I neither heard nor saw any boats. I walked downriver, along the bank, as far as I could. But after about a quarter of a mile, the banks became so steep that I had to head up a worn path to a ridge overlooking the river.

From there I could see the top of walls enclosing another tight little canyon, and could hear the flow of some stream separate from the Colorado itself. I noticed a path to the right, and I followed it down and dropped into a wash, where I found a small, steady stream of water making its way down towards the river. This tiny stream has cut itself a channel in the rock, so narrow that it was necessary, at places, to wade. It was sort of fun, for the water is warm. A few bends in the canyon, a couple of small two- to three-foot waterfalls and I was at the bottom of a waterfall and an eighteen-foot metal ladder.

These hot springs get a lot of use, in the warmer months, from people arriving by boat. There are other hot springs upriver, such as the popular Gold Strike and Boy Scout, both located on the Nevada shore. It's hard to hike to Gold Strike Hot Springs now because con-

ARIZONA

Colorado River

NEVADA

93

Designated route

Alternate route

Ringbolt Rapids

■ Arizona Hot Springs

1 mile

Getting there

Location: Arizona Hot Springs, in Lake Mead National Recreation Area, about 36 miles from Las Vegas.

Directions: From Las Vegas take U.S. 93 south over Hoover Dam. Drive 4.2 miles past the dam and take a right turn into parking area.

Season: October through April for hiking from U.S. 93. Visiting by boat is practical the year around.

Length: 5.6 miles round trip.

Elevation at trailhead: 1,570 feet.

Elevation loss/gain: 800 feet.

Difficulty: Moderate.

Water: Colorado River, treat before drinking. Do not take water from hot springs.

Hazards: *Naegleria fowleria*, an amoeba, may be present; do not submerge your head or splash water. Flash flooding, rattlesnakes and hard-to-find alternative route.

Parental advisory: Nude bathers are sometimes encountered, even though National Park Service discourages nudity.

Camping: Dispersed camping allowed. Boulder Campground has 154 sites at $10 per night, first come, first served. Located off Lakeshore Scenic Drive not far from Alan Bible Visitor Center on Nevada side of Lake Mead.

Lake Mead National Recreation Area: No fees for accessing this part of the recreation area. Alan Bible Visitor Center is open daily 8:30 a.m.-4:30 p.m. except Thanksgiving, Christmas and New Years Day, (702) 293-8990, **www.nps.gov/lame.**

Topographic Maps: Trails Illustrated-Lake Mead National Recreation Area 1:145,728. For more detail use USGS Ringbolt Rapids, 1:24,000. Both are available at the visitor center or **mapping.usgs.gov.**

struction crews working on the Hoover Dam bypass have temporarily blocked off the trailhead. But it's still easy to get to the Nevada springs by boat, traveling up river from Willow Beach, on the Arizona shore.

Having seen no boats on the river and an empty parking area at the trailhead, I assumed I would find the spring unoccupied. But when I climbed up the metal ladder, I found Mike Henry soaking in the first pool.

He had arrived at the trailhead after me, but had taken the alternate route down and said he arrived about twenty minutes before me.

He told me there were more pools above, so I let him enjoy his solitude and continued upstream. The second pool was just a few yards farther and about two feet deep, about 25 feet long. The third was half that size. All three pools owe their depth to manmade dams of sandbags.

Just above the third pool, a heavy flow of water poured out of the rock face like water from a bathtub faucet. When I placed my hand under the flow, the temperature was so hot I couldn't stand it more than a few seconds. I had packed along a home medical thermometer to measure the temperature, but its scale went no higher than 106, and I am guessing this fountain reached 120.

A National Park Service publication says that water is heated deep within the earth by molten rock and then moves to the surface through faults, at temperatures from 85 to 120 degrees Farenheit, at an overall rate of 400 gallons per minute. Of course it is heavily mineralized.

I headed up around the bend and found an eight-foot cliff blocking farther progress. Cool water flowed from this cliff.

Returning to the pools, I measured the temperatures in all three. The top one was a hot 106, the next 103, and Henry's pool 98. The 103-degree pool was the best for me and I soaked for a while, thinking it was pretty close to paradise, having my own private hot tub in this primitive setting.

Henry told me the sandbags are occasionally moved around by visitors to achieve different depths, pool shapes and temperatures. Apparently, night visiting is popular too, because solidified candle wax can be found all over the canyon walls, below small crevices and ledges that serve as candleholders. It is pleasant to soak in the mineral waters while looking at the stars; in fact, the

Warm water tumbles over a dam at Arizona Hot Springs. They've been a popular hiking destination since the '30s, when workers were building Hoover Dam.
(BY ALAN ROBERTS)

narrow canyon walls shut out so much light from the sides, that it is sometimes possible to see stars in the daytime.

I knew there was another route back but hadn't done it myself. Since Mike was leaving about the same time as me, I asked if he would mind if I tagged along. I was confident he would show me the right way since he has traveled the route close to one hundred times.

If you don't have any children along, and you are up to handling a few tough scrambles and able to follow a topographic map, this would be the preferred route. But neither the park service nor your narrator recommends it otherwise, for the trail markings are confusing, and it really would be easy to miss the route.

That said, Henry even showed me some nice petroglyph panels, and some shortcuts around some of those tough scrambling areas. Hiking this alternate route proved very satisfying — but don't pass up that soak in the gravy boat. ◆

Alan Roberts of Las Vegas has frequently published outdoor photographs in Cerca.

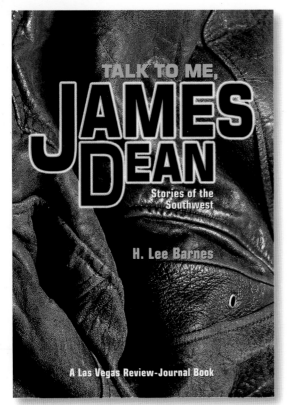

Talk to Me, James Dean

H. Lee Barnes

A new collection of short stories played out on the landscape of the American Southwest, by the author of *Gunning for Ho* and *Dummy Up and Deal*. Barnes has forged dead-accurate characters who are looking for love while trying to maintain sanity and honor in a world that seems short on all three.

ISBN 1-932173-16-1 ~ $21.95
Hardcover

Gary Ladd's Canyon Light: Lake Powell and the Grand Canyon

Many never-before-published photos of Lake Powell and the Grand Canyon, stretching more than 400 miles along the Colorado River, by renowned Southwest photographer Gary Ladd, who has been seriously photographing the area for 30 years! Gary shares insightful tips on photography, reveals his philosophy through many of the photos, and offers a brief explanation of natural history captured by his camera.

ISBN 1-932173-01-3 ~ $34.95
Hardcover

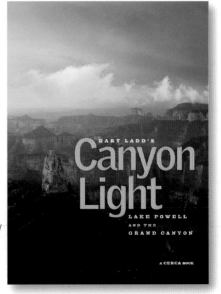

BOOKS FOR AND ABOUT THE SOUTHWEST

Order Online: www.stephenspress.com

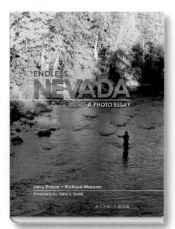

Endless Nevada

Beautiful photo/essay coffee table book about Nevada. Photographs by noted Nevada photographer Larry Prosor and essays written by *Nevada Magazine* publisher Richard Moreno.

ISBN 1-932173-03-X ~ $34.95
Hardcover

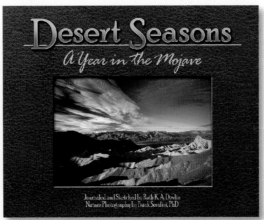

Desert Seasons: A Year in the Mojave

Ruth K.A. Devlin and Frank Serafini, Ph.D

A journal for all ages to appreciate and learn about our mighty Mojave Desert and its seasons of nature. Magnificent photography and thoughtful journaling, interspersed with interesting facts, present desert life in all its glory.

ISBN 1-932173-18-8 ~ $17.95
Hardcover

Tomás the Tortoise Adventure Series
One Hot Day • Play in the Clouds Joshua's Surprise

Curious Tomás, a resident of Red Rock Canyon, is joined by many desert friends on adventures while young readers and listeners learn about the Mojave Desert and its environs. In *One Hot Day*, he sets out at sunrise on a trek to Lake Mead. *Play in the Clouds* finds a determined Tomás climbing to the snowy heights of Mount Charleston. In *Joshua's Surprise*, the plucky tortoise's holiday exuberance softens even the hard heart of a spiky old Joshua tree.

These beautifully illustrated stories are destined to become classics for desert-dwelling children.

$15.95 each ~ All three $39.95
Hardcover

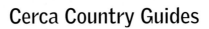

Cerca Country Guides

Collect these themed editions about the great outdoors in Cerca Country. Each soft-cover book covers a different subject with first-person accounts, detailed travel information and astounding photography. Look for titles on great weekend trips and more.

$11.95 each
Softcover ~ Issued Quarterly

Stephens Press

P.O. BOX 1600
LAS VEGAS, NV 89125
(800) 473-2737